I
WORKED FOR
THE SOVIET

By

Countess Alexandra Tolstoy

Translated by the Author
In Collaboration with Roberta Yerkes

New Haven
YALE UNIVERSITY PRESS
1934

Contents

CONTENTS

I Worked for the Soviet

I

1917

A PLUMP face with rosy cheeks and a small birdlike nose bent over me. This nurse with her shiny face and perpetual smile irritated me. She had been sent from the detachment to the hospital at Minsk to take care of me. I was sick with pyæmia, I had been operated on, my temperature was high, and my head giddy.

But the Revolution had just broken out, and the uncertainty of the political situation worried me much more than the pain of the wound. Why was the nurse so happy? Her white teeth sparkled. Her small merry gray eyes almost disappeared in the creases of her fat cheeks.

The surgeon, an elderly Jew, came and sat by my bed and counted my pulse.

"Well, Doctor, how are things?"

"The infection is all right, but the malaria gives you a high temperature."

"No, I don't mean that. Has the Revolution gone any further?"

"Yes, the Grand Duke Michael Alexandrovich has refused the throne."

"Oh! That means . . . it looks as if . . . Now Russia is lost."

"Yes, Russia is lost," the doctor repeated sadly as he left the room. The nurse smiled stupidly.

I LEFT the hospital before my wound was healed. The doctor said I was crazy but he let me go. In March, 1917, when the snow was melting and the roads were very bad, I went back to the front.

Since 1916 I had been in charge of a large hospital unit, consisting of three detachments and a base a few miles in the rear where we had our headquarters and stored our forage and provisions. Each detachment had a commander, two doctors, five nurses, about a hundred men and one hundred and thirty horses. Our job was to give first aid to the sick and wounded and transport them farther to the rear.

Nothing had changed with the Revolution. The soldiers stayed on in the trenches, lazily exchanging bullets now and then with the Germans. In the rear, life went on as usual. The men cut wood, heated their mud huts, and stood duty. Only, instead of calling the officers "Your Honor" and "Your Excellency," they began using the absurd and not less bourgeois "Mr. Colonel," and "Mr. General." In some regiments the officers themselves took off their epaulettes; in others, the soldiers tore them off. As before, the hospital detachments, having little to do, were bored and listless; and the officers continued to flirt with the nurses.

Yet officers, doctors, nurses, the zemstvo workers—everybody —pretended that with the change in government we had a group of intelligent people at the head of our country instead of Nicholas II, and that everything was utterly changed. Officers and men forsook the Tsar. There were no monarchists left in the army. The officers were suddenly very polite to the soldiers, calling them "you" instead of "thou," and adding "please" to their orders.

And I who had awaited a more liberal government for many years, one without militarism, and with religious and political freedom, and with land for the peasants, watched these changes with mixed feelings. Like other Russian liberals, I had considered an overthrow of the monarchy essential, but felt that it should not come until after the war. With the Grand Duke Michael's refusal of the throne, and the war going on, anything might happen.

"THE soldiers are waiting for you," the commander said. "When do you wish to speak to them?" The soldiers had never asked me to speak to them before. I realized that I, too, must behave differently.

"I'll do it now. Call the men together."

"Good morning, men," I said as I entered the barracks, packed with soldiers.

"Good morning, Madam Representative," they answered. They said it just like that: "Madam Representative."

"Citizens!" I began, "in this short time, Russia has passed through great events. The Russian people have torn off the chains of the old tsarist tyranny . . ."

For some reason I was ashamed of myself, though the words I was saying seemed to be the right ones and I went on talking. When I had nothing more to say:

"Hurrah!" I shouted. "Hurrah! Long live free Russia!"

"Hurrah!" shouted the soldiers. They surrounded me and wanted to toss me in the air. I could already feel the pain of my wound. The chief of the detachment hurried to my rescue, and the soldiers tossed him.

"Will you allow us to ask you, Madam Representative," the chairman of the soldiers' committee said, "why the detachment is going to be moved?"

"It is the order of the chief of the division."

"Will you allow me to suggest that it would have been a good idea to let the committee of the detachment see the place and consult us on the matter?"

The idea of collectivism was being instilled. We could no longer ignore it.

The new location was examined by five persons. We rode about on horseback, looking for something better. We argued and discussed and lost five days, but we could not find anything more suitable than the place the commander had chosen. It was safe and quiet.

No sooner were we settled in the valley between two steep hills than the Germans opened fire. About two o'clock in the

morning a familiar sound wakened me. Cannon were rolling. One after another heavy shells screamed over our heads. The men awoke, their excited voices echoed in the stillness of the night, horses clanked the chains of their tethers, and our big spotted dog "Grouse" began to howl. A few shells plunked into the opposite bank, splashing a fountain of dirt around. The men ran in scattered groups toward the blindage.

"What? Abandoning the sick and wounded, you scoundrels!" the commandant shouted, forgetting the new politeness.

It was impossible to stop them. Neither anger nor reason had any effect.

Down the hill, from neighboring regiments, soldiers in white shirts and drawers were running to our hollow.

"Brothers!" one of them shouted. "Brothers! save yourselves!"

In the red-yellow glow of the coming dawn, over the foggy dimness of the woods, a large black spot surrounded by smaller spots appeared and drew nearer. Looking like swallows, they flew over us toward the German front—a big Sikorski surrounded by small Farmans.

Open-mouthed and slowly turning their heads, the soldiers watched the planes till they disappeared. Suddenly the cannonade stopped. One by one the men returned to their regiments. There was something infinitely weak and miserable in those white barefooted figures slowly climbing the hill.

In July, on the Western front near Krevo, an enormous army was concentrated against the Germans. Troops and batteries were hidden in every thicket. Never in my life had I experienced such fire. Cannon roared day and night. We could not speak or hear each other. Guns burst from the terrific heat. New ones were brought and ammunition caissons traveled at all hours.

We had but few wounded, and most of these were invalids and officers. The soldiers were leaving the front in large numbers.

"Will you take care of me? And be quick about it" . . . a soldier poked his wounded finger into the nurse's face.

"Please wait, comrade, we've got some that are wounded much more seriously than you are."

"But I tell you you must take care of me."

"I cannot, I have orders."

"You bitches! Bandage my finger, I say, or I'll . . ."

"What's the matter? What's the noise about?" the surgeon inquired, coming out of the ambulance tent, his clean hands in the air. "The worst cases first—head, stomach, chest!" He disappeared into the tent. The soldier cursed.

It was said that seven lines of German barbed wire and trenches had been swept away by the shelling. The Germans retreated. But the Bolshevik propaganda kept on.

"Germans, comrades! Look out! German cavalry!" men shouted as the Germans were seen wheeling off with their limbers. The soldiers ran. By evening the Russian troops which had moved forward easily earlier in the day had retreated to their former positions.

A BOY officer sat in the dining room of our detachment. He covered his face with his hands and wept. "Oh, the beasts, the beasts!"

"Who?"

"The soldiers. What swine! I never knew they were such swine! My best friend was shot down. Every one of the officers . . . and my best friend. Oh! but it's not that. I wish I'd been killed! Do you know how he died? Those devils! They left the machine gun and ran. He was wounded in the foot. He crawled up to the gun, pressed the button and kept on firing. The second shell killed him. What do you think of a death like that? And do you know what they said? I heard them. 'The war must be profitable to the officers. Even when they get wounded, those servants of the bourgeoisie still go on fighting!' The devils!" And the boy officer started weeping again.

A STREAM of curses. Everybody started up. One of the nurses

shrieked. "You bastards!!! You're . . .!" A heavy fist hit the table with enormous strength. The dishes clattered and one of the cups belonging to the woman doctor bounced off and fell to the floor, and again the frightened medical staff started.

The steward, a Pole, jumped up and approached the soldier with an amiable smile. In prerevolutionary days he might have smacked his face, but he was polite now:

"What's the matter with you, comrade?" he asked. "Please calm yourself, I beg you . . ."

"By God! Sending me at night with the wounded! You're warm—drinking tea . . ."

A grayish face, spattered with clay as gray as his coat, trembling lips, a quivering chin, and running eyes.

"Stop. We'll talk about it tomorrow," I said, putting my hand on the cuff of the coarse coat and looking into his dark blue eyes. Suddenly he shriveled, and became confused, small and pitiful.

"The cart turned over. I couldn't get out, the horses dragged me in the mud, my foot got caught in the reins. . . . I'm dog tired. . . . How can you send us out so late at night?" He burst out again. "The wounded should be moved in the daytime!"

And banging the door, he went out, leaving clumps of mud on the floor. The neat little nurse-housekeeper picked up the broken pieces of the cup and wiped the floor with a mop.

"His brain isn't quite right," said the surgeon. "He's been hit on the head. The men said he had those fits once in a while. He nearly killed someone with an ax in a fight."

"This is just the beginning," the Pole grumbled. "If that fellow knew he'd be punished for abusing his superiors, he wouldn't have any brain trouble, believe me. There's no discipline."

"Anyhow," the woman doctor suggested, "we must get rid of the man. He is dangerous not only for us, but for the sick."

"We'll try and send him to the front," said the Pole. "We can't have such behavior."

"I was frightened to death. I thought he'd kill us all," said the pretty nurse with curly dark hair over her forehead, looking sideways at the surgeon, with whom she was usually flirting. "Why didn't you stop him, Nikolay Petrovich? Were you afraid, too?"

"Oh, no! But you must never irritate a person who is mentally ill. . . . Let's have a game of chess."

The air was close and suffocating. Our talk, too, was flat and dull. Outdoors the wind was blowing, gusts of rain were beating against the windows. And in the dark, crowded barracks a new power that had been checked for ages was growing. It was rising with dreadful force, sometimes exploding in ugly fantastic forms; it had been suppressed so long that nothing could hold it down now.

I talked with the soldier the next day. "What the devil did we have the Revolution for?" he asked. "Instead of Nicholas II, we've got Lvovs and Kerenskys. Nothing's changed. We're still feeding lice in the trenches."

He spoke rapidly, swallowing his words, breathing heavily, as if afraid he would not have time to say all he wanted to. "It's all just the same. Your little Pole is drinking tea, maybe wine, in a warm room, and I . . . Am I worse than he is? I haven't seen my wife and children for more than a year. . . ."

The man wept like a child, rubbing his eyes with his dirty fist and smearing the dirt all over his face.

"Where's the truth, where is it? The surgeon's assistant says: 'You've fought enough with the Germans. Now you fellows go home and fight the bourgeois. Take the land from the landowners and the factories from the capitalists!' And our commander says: 'Cowards! Why do you swallow all that nonsense? Can't you understand you're betraying your country? The duty of every soldier is to stand up for Russia till his last breath, till the victorious end.' Oh, where's the truth, where is it? I don't know."

II

TALK

THE barracks were crowded. Two dim kerosene lamps were burning at each end. The fumes of cheap tobacco mingled with the smell of cabbage soup and onions.

At the detachment base about fifteen miles from the front, the first election of the delegates for the Constituent Assembly was taking place. The chief of the base, a curly-haired, freckled young man, smoked nervously, his knotted fingers trembling slightly. He was popular among the soldiers and we all thought that he would be chosen, but we were mistaken. A soldier who took care of the warehouse, Bormin,[1] was elected. The soldiers couldn't have done better. Bormin was an honest, serious man. The other candidate was as good.

The whole atmosphere of the assembly was businesslike and serious, as if the soldiers were entirely used to voting.

"Comrades!" Bormin said in his calm, gentle voice. "Forgive me, but I can't, really I can't. It's no joke to be a delegate . . . you have to be educated and smart, and what am I? Just a peasant who only went to primary school. No education, no experience! I can't, comrades, excuse me."

The soldiers urged him, but he would not change his mind. "It's no joke to be a delegate, I can't."

"Well, then, Bolotov will be our delegate, he's next."

"Oh, no, comrades. I thank you heartily, comrades. If a man like Bormin refuses, how can I accept? I'm nearly illiterate! I can't!"

Dismay, confusion, almost horror were in the man's face, in his very figure, as he stood there tense and strained, at attention. His wide round face with light whiskers and eyebrows was scarlet.

"You've got to, Comrade Bolotov," one of the soldiers

---

[1] I have thought it best to give fictitious names to many of the people who appear in this book.

shouted. "We trust you. If everybody refuses, what will we do?"

"You're foolish, Bolotov!" another soldier cried. "If you fellows had chosen me, I wouldn't have refused!"

But Bolotov would not consent. "I can't, upon my word of honor, I can't. I haven't got . . . I can't talk. . . . Well, I don't know how to explain it, but I haven't got the courage to try. I just can't—and that's all."

There was an uproar in the barracks. For a few minutes no one could make himself heard. The curly-headed young man tried to bring the assembly to order.

"Sukman! Let's have Sukman, the clerk," a loud voice cried.

Somebody laughed. Sukman sat motionless, as if the matter did not concern him in the least. He was busy writing down the proceedings of the assembly. He was always like that, paying no attention to what was going on around him, bent over his desk, writing in his clear round hand.

"But he's got only three votes."

"But if everybody else refuses?"

"He's a Jew. We want a Russian delegate."

"Shame on you, comrades. We've got freedom and equality nowadays," the same voice insisted. "Sukman! We want Sukman to be our delegate!"

The soldiers were silent. Suddenly and unexpectedly, putting his pen behind his right ear, Sukman rose.

"Comrades, I will be your delegate! Thank you for the honor, comrades!" He was silent for a moment, took the pen from behind his ear, started to sit down, then all at once straightened up, his black eyes shining, and cried out, raising his voice strangely: "Com-rades! I shall defend the interests of the proletariat to the last drop of my bloooood!"

Then he became calm and silent again. His small dark head, and body in a neat, clean suit tightened with a new yellow belt, bent over the minutes of the proceedings.

The assembly was closed. The next day, a new clerk was doing the work in the office, and delegate Sukman started for Minsk.

EVERYBODY was making speeches. Platforms sprouted like mushrooms. There were meetings everywhere. Strangers—all sorts of extraordinary people—appeared and urged the soldiers not to submit to the officers but to leave the front. Officers, soldiers, nurses, everybody made speeches. I went to a detachment and found myself taking part in a meeting. A Bolshevik agitator was on the tribune. He had scarcely finished before my chauffeur jumped on the platform.

"Comrades," he cried, as if he had done nothing but deliver speeches all his life, "comrades, I am a Pole, but I am a Russian patriot. I am for the continuation of the war until the victorious end with no annexations or indemnities." He ejaculated short, loud sentences and struck his chest. When he had finished, the soldiers shouted "Hurrah!" They were going to toss him in the air, but a new speaker sprang to the platform.

"Down with the spongers of capital!" he shouted at the top of his voice. "Down with the bloodsuckers who are drinking the blood of the working class! While you soldiers are feeding lice in the trenches, while you are damp, hungry, cold, and miserable, the Tsar's spies, avoiding military service for their own selfish ends, are trying to . . ."

He spoke for about half an hour. "Long live the Council of the Soldiers' and Workers' Deputies!" he concluded.

"Hurrah!" the soldiers roared, and, seizing the speaker awkwardly by his hands and feet, they flung him into the air.

I felt something boiling in my breast. I could bear it no longer. I, too, was standing on the platform delivering a patriotic speech.

It was madness.

I shall never forget a division commander, an old Bulgarian general. It was said that his body was covered with scars; that he had once been flogged in his native country for his revolutionary activities. He spoke very calmly but wholeheartedly of the necessity for holding the front, of our duty to the new revolutionary government. When he finished, there were tears in his eyes and the soldiers, too, were moved. But at the first sounds of a new shrill-voiced speaker, the impression of his quiet words disappeared.

Anger, hatred, vengeance were beating on strained nerves, awaking powerful, long-suppressed waves of independence and rage.

"Down with the Tsar's generals! United into one peaceful front, the proletariat of the whole world will repulse all the capitalists and hangmen of the world! Comrades! Down with the war against our brothers! Let us begin building a peaceful socialist life. Peace to the huts! War to the palaces!"

Those were new, not quite understandable, words, but they burned like fire. They were a call to something unknown, un-experienced, and certainly something better than tsarism.

The general bent his white head as if he had suddenly be-come very old and weak, and making strange short sounds through his nose, walked slowly away.

ONCE, as I drove up to the quarters of the first detachment, the doctors and the commander rushed excitedly out of the tent to meet me.

"Please let us take your automobile! They're having a meet-ing three miles from here and Kerensky is going to speak!"

I wanted to hear him, too, and we all jumped into the car.

We were late. A crowd of soldiers was collected. On a high tribune a slender man in a soldier's khaki coat was shouting words that were scarcely distinguishable. He was very hoarse. But I thought I detected an artificial emotion in the words I caught.

As we drove home and the doctors exchanged enthusiastic banal talk about the speech, I was bored and anxious.

"Can people seriously believe," I thought, "that this hoarse man can save Russia with his speeches?"

AN inspection consisting of the division veterinary, a general, and representatives from the zemstvo came to the first detach-ment to examine the horses. At that time, because of lack of discipline and care, many of the horses in the army were infected with mange. But in all our three detachments we had succeeded in avoiding the disease. I gave an order to the commander of the detachment, who passed it on to the sergeant major, as military procedure required, for the horses to be brought to the front door by the soldiers. Five, ten, twenty minutes passed. The inspectors were waiting. I had begun to feel a little nervous, when the commander came in and asked to see me privately. The sergeant major reported that the soldiers refused to bring up the horses.

"What! Send the sergeant to me."

"What's the matter? Why don't you bring the horses?" I asked him.

"The soldiers say that if the general wants to see the horses, he can come to the line and look at them."

Pretending not to hear or quite understand the sergeant major, I said sternly, "I don't like this at all. You are keeping the inspectors waiting. You know that our horses are in good shape and that there is nothing to be worried about. Tell the men that everything will be all right. The other horses have mange but ours are in fine condition. Four gallons of wine if the inspectors are pleased."

"But, Madam Representative . . ."

"Don't you understand me? Now hurry. The horses must be here in five minutes, and don't forget to give the order about the wine for the men."

"Yes, Madam Representative."

In five minutes the men came up in fine order, each leading his well-fed, healthy team. The general was pleased.

"Very good, men!"

"Glad to carry out your orders, Mr. General!"

Everybody cheered up. The soldiers began to smile good naturedly.

But on the whole the situation became more complicated every day. Discipline was breaking up. It was especially bad in the second detachment. The commander could not do anything with the soldiers. They insolently refused to work. They would not move to a new location ordered by the commander of the division. Part of the reason for this was that the surgeon of the unit happened to be a Bolshevik, and the woman doctor of the second detachment was infatuated not only with the doctor's ideas but with the doctor himself. There was also a Bolshevik nurse in the detachment who was spreading Communist propaganda among the soldiers.

Everywhere discipline was going down rapidly. During an inspection of the troops, the commander of the division visited a military detachment. Nobody met him. He walked into the barracks; the men were lying on their boards and barely answered his greeting. The old general was astonished when he found that in our detachment, which was not a military organization, the soldiers stood at attention and were polite, but he never knew how we had worked for that.

Communist propaganda spread through the second detachment like a plague. The soldiers stopped working, stopped grooming the horses; everything was dirty and in disorder. Unable to bear it any longer I disbanded the detachment. There was little more to do at the front and, in fact, the war was really over. The soldiers were either fraternizing with the enemy or deserting. I decided to give up the whole unit. I turned it over to a naïve man who thought that work could still be accomplished, and I left for Moscow.

THE committee of all the detachments decided to have a farewell meeting in my honor. The chairman delivered a weighty speech.

"Comrades!" he said. "Today, we are seeing off our highly honored representative, who has been working so hard for our native, I mean our revolutionary, country! Comrades! Our detachment, the third detachment of the zemstvo unit is really the best one. Comrades! Why is that so? I'll explain it, comrades. In all the other detachments they haven't got enough food for the men and for the horses. We've got plenty. The people and the animals are all satisfied. And why is that, comrades? It is because our representative . . ." and so on and on.

At last he concluded:

"Comrades! I wish our representative good luck and a happy journey, and I ask you to stand up in memory of our representative."

Everyone rose, as they do in Russia when someone has died.

Later I learned that this same committee which thanked me so politely and solemnly decided to arrest me as a bourgeois and counterrevolutionary. But it was too late. I had started for Moscow.

"VASKA, you devil, come on, I tell you!"

Raising one shoulder, a soldier bent, and with exaggerated jauntiness slung his bag on the plush seat of the train. A timid, freckled face appeared from behind the door.

"But this is the first-class compartment, isn't it? Won't they turn us out?"

"They won't, I tell you, you fool! Come on! That's all over. Now it's our turn to throw the bourgeois out. . . ." And the soldier looked at me.

"Grand!" said Vaska, bouncing up and down on the springs. "The bourgeois certainly knew how to travel!"

"They're through now! You, lady, move! We want to make ourselves comfortable."

There was no place to move to. I was sitting in the very corner. The soldier stretched out on the seat and pushed me with his dirty boots. I was going to get out when he jumped up and rushed into the corridor. The train had just left Minsk. There was a terrible racket in the aisle—yelling, swearing, the sound of breaking glass.

"Oho, ho, ho! Fine! That's the way to do it!" the soldier shouted. "They've sucked enough of our blood."

I looked out into the corridor. It was full of soldiers. Vaska stood with his mouth open, watching attentively.

"What's the matter?" I asked.

"Well, they've thrown an officer's luggage out the window.

And I shouldn't be surprised if the officer followed. The boys look pretty mad."

I went back to my place in the corner, wishing I could throw out the whole carload, with their dirty boots and their insolence—especially this first loutish soldier with the boots. I was to have the pleasure of his company for two days.

The train sped on. Gathering his blouse in his hand, Vaska came in, scratching his chest.

"Well, that fellow is lucky," he said. "They left him alone, but I don't know how he did it. I'd have bet they'd throw him out, too!"

"Why are you standing?" I asked. "Sit down. Will you have a cigarette?"

With dirty, rough fingers, Vaska awkwardly pulled a cigarette from my case and sat down.

"What province are you from?"

"Tula."

"Oh! Then, we're fellow countrymen. I'm from Tula province, too."

"What district?"

Vaska was going home. He was happy. He wanted to tell me everything about himself, his family, his young wife. In about twenty minutes I knew his whole story. We were so absorbed that we did not notice the other soldier come in.

"Vaska, have you got any tobacco?"

"No."

I handed him my cigarette case. Silently, without thanking me, he took a cigarette.

"Now, look here!" I said. "We have a long journey ahead of us. There's no use being disagreeable to each other. I have a kettle, tea, sugar, and food. One of you can fetch hot water from the next station and we'll have tea. Stop swearing, and we'll try to make things pleasant."

"Sure!" Vaska said. His friend was silent, but when the train stopped, he took the kettle and brought boiling water from the station.

At every station more soldiers got into the train. The compartments were jammed. Men sat, stood, lay in the corridor, so that if you wanted to get out, you had to climb through the window. My kettle was handed from one to another. The soldiers got out their tin mugs, and, blowing on their fingers, sipped hot tea. No one tried to insult me. It seemed to be understood that I was one of the party. They tried not to curse, but they smoked all the time and spat on the floor.

Before night, I got out at a station. The soldiers helped me to climb back through the window.

"Oh! the devil! Isn't she fat?" a soldier shouted, leaning out of the window of the compartment and pulling me up by the hands with all his strength. "Climb in, I tell you! Now then! Uhh!"

"Wait, wait a moment!" Vaska shrieked in his high tenor. "I'll boost her, there's plenty to push."

"Be careful, you fool! She'll break your back, she will!"

When we arrived at Moscow, the soldiers helped me carry my baggage to a cab.

"Goodbye, sister!" they shouted as I drove away, "good luck, good health to you!"

III

HOMELESS

I REACHED Moscow in November, 1917. The fighting had just stopped, and the Whites had been beaten. But, strange to say, although everyone I met sympathized with the Whites, no one seemed depressed. On the contrary, everyone was animated. The people of Moscow, who during the war had been well in the rear of the armies, were excited by gun-fire. They were more concerned about someone's running out in the street during a battle, or about having to break into a store and eat caviar with large spoons to keep from starving, than about the issue of the battle or the future of Russia. The Bolsheviks and the Council of the Soldiers' and Workers' Deputies seemed so insignificant that it was absurd to be worried over Russia. It never occurred to anybody that they would hold power for long. Events followed each other with astonishing rapidity, and we felt sure that Bolshevism would be a transient thing, gone in a few weeks or perhaps months. Everyone I met was of the same opinion.

None of us knew what was going to happen or what we were going to do. Some were still trying to save their money, others to save themselves. The Bolsheviks were arresting and shooting people, but with a certain discretion. They were not at all sure themselves that they would be able to keep in power. Radicalism seemed to mean something in those days. A person involved in one way or another in revolutionary activity under the old *régime* could be saved from persecution.

Opposite my home in Moscow were the ruins of what had been a large stone house. There were signs of recent fighting— battered houses and tumbled walls—on every side. The house where I had lived was still standing, but my room was empty of personal belongings: everything was gone except a few pieces of furniture. The White and the Red staffs had lodged there alternately.

I tried to save the money I had in the bank, but that was a waste of time. The banks were nationalized and I lost nearly everything I owned. In the excitement I felt neither terror nor disappointment, but only relief, as though I had taken off a shuba[1] which had been warm but had weighed heavily on my shoulders. Loss of property meant very little in comparison with one's loss of inner balance. How were we going to live? Why should we live? The Bolsheviks proclaimed the destruction of the old life. The Revolution was sweeping everything before it, declaring proudly that a new world was to be built. What was to become of the old world in the process?

I could find no place for myself. Life was empty and weary, and any kind of creative work was choked. I waited as everybody waited. But meanwhile I had to think of earning my living. I had received a month's salary from the zemstvo when I left the front, and on this I got along for a few months. Rooms were to be had free or for a very low rent immediately after the nationalization of houses; railroad passes were free to workers; and clothes were simply not to be found. Food was my greatest need. People said that it was easy to get a job as a bookkeeper. I loathe figures and bookkeeping, but what did that matter? For a while I studied debit and credit conscientiously. But that did not last long. I soon threw the books away. Friends tried to get me into political activity; that was not my *métier,* either. Politics had always seemed to me among the worst inventions of mankind.

At about ten one night, as I was thinking of going to bed, someone knocked at the door.

"Come in!"

A tall, very dark man in a black cassock entered. I noticed at once his large bright eyes and his pallid face, which seemed paler because of his black beard.

"I am Bishop ——," he said.

I looked at him in amazement—what could I do for him? His name was well known. I had heard of his remarkable

---

[1] Fur coat.

work in the far north. I got up, but did not ask for a blessing and did not kiss his hand as Orthodox custom required. I simply shook hands with him. He smiled as if to say, "I did not expect anything else."

"No one will hear us?" he asked, looking around.

"No. I am alone in the attic. Don't worry."

He sat down and again looked around, still hesitating. I did not break the silence. I watched him. There was nothing holy about him. He looked strong and ardent, and he was handsome, too. "Women must be crazy about him," I thought.

He began speaking in a solemn whisper, looking me in the eyes, trying to impress me as one does who is used to being admired. He spoke of the salvation of Russia, of our duty to unite no matter what our ideas or religion, for the sake of Russia.

His eyes sparkled, his speech was brilliant and convincing.

"Wouldn't you make a sacrifice for your country? Even risk your life?" he whispered.

"Perhaps, if it were not against my conscience," I answered. "What do you want me to do?"

"Would you help us even if it were very dangerous?"

"Tell me, Father, what this is all about, and I will answer you frankly."

"You see," he began hesitatingly, "our anti-Bolshevist group has decided that the only thing we can do now to save Russia is to restore the monarchy. It is certain that if the family of the Tsar remains in the hands of the Bolsheviks, they will all be massacred. We have made up our minds to kidnap the Tsarevich. We will keep him abroad, say in England. And at the right moment, we will declare to the people that the Grand Duke Alexis is alive and will be proclaimed Tsar. The people will follow us. Can you help us plan the kidnapping of the Grand Duke Alexis?"

I had expected anything, yet I was so thunderstruck that for some time I could not say a word. For a moment his contagious madness got hold of me and I really considered the idea. I always liked adventure, and this was one such as I had never dreamed of. But that was only for a few seconds. My thoughts returned to the rut of common sense. Without taking his black eyes off my face, the bishop waited for me to speak.

"I cannot, Father, I cannot. . . ."

What help would there be in a sick, delicate boy, even if he were on the Russian throne? The Russians had suffered too much these last years. They did not need the reëstablishment of the old *régime*. The mistakes of Tsarism and the Orthodox church had prepared the soil for the Bolshevik Revolution, and it was absurd to think of restoring that same government.

The bishop went, leaving me an enormous package of proclamations. I looked them over. They were appeals to the people, written in a bad monarchic-orthodox style. I burned them and stopped thinking about politics.

It was not easy to give up my country home,[2] which was declared government property. The members of the village Soviet had come and laid claim to what they wanted—horses, cows, machinery, and tools. I could not realize that my house and the horses and dogs I had raised and trained myself no longer belonged to me.

I went through the cold empty rooms. Long before I returned from the front, thieves had got in and stolen furniture and clothes and dishes. I could not bear the sight of the place. I visited the servants' quarters and the barn, and talked with the workers. Nothing interested me; nothing was mine. I went into the garden and sat on a bench. Two large white Eskimo dogs that I had raised from puppies ran to me, looking in my face, licking my hands.

"What shall I do with them?" I thought. "Take them with me? Where?"

For the first time it was borne in upon me that I did not have a home any more.

I had to get it over with, and the sooner the better—give up my house, but not the animals. I called the estate manager. He

---

[2] My own house at Novaia Poliana, three miles from the Tolstoy estate at Yasnaia Poliana.

had been platoon commander in my detachment at the front—
a silent, businesslike Ukrainian. His small brown eyes squinted,
and his drooping mustache could not hide his cunning half-
smile.

"Harness all the horses to the carts."

He stood before me as silent and stubborn as only a Ukrainian can be.

"Harness the horses," I repeated, getting angry.

"But may we?"

"May we what?"

"The village Soviet forbade anyone's taking anything away."

"It's not your business to argue about it!" I said. "Harness
up. I'll be responsible for whatever happens."

He was used to obeying my orders. "All right."

With the help of the workers who were still on the estate, we
loaded the carts with machinery, tools, beehives, and furniture,
and drove to the old Tolstoy home at Yasnaia Poliana. As soon
as the carts were unloaded, we went back for more. We
worked all day. The workers shook their heads and laughed,
but did not object.

I slept in the empty house on a pile of hay, and next morning about three o'clock, in the darkness, we took the horses to
market and sold them for half what they were worth. But I
was happy at not having left them for the village Soviet.

Then I went to the department of agriculture. A section had
just been established to protect thoroughbred animals. Peasants
were taking over great properties and farms with purebred
cattle, and, not knowing what to do with them, they simply
killed stallions and bulls that had cost thousands of rubles. A
peasant would try to harness a thoroughbred trotter to his cart.
The harness wouldn't fit, the horse would be nervous, and the
cart would get smashed and the horse hurt. One peasant got a
stallion which had won a number of prizes at the races; but his
stable was too small for the huge animal. Not knowing what
else to do with it, he killed it.

The chief of the section, whom I had known before, came

and marked my cows and bull as thoroughbred cattle belonging to the Agricultural Department of Tula, so that no one had
the right to kill them or dispose of them.

There was nothing more to be done. I whistled to the dogs
and drove off to Yasnaia Poliana with the last horse that was
left, the dogs joyfully following.

My mother, my sister Tania with her little daughter Tanichka,
and my aunt lived at Yasnaia Poliana. All the neighboring estates were in ashes and nearly every house in our district had
been robbed and burned. There had been rumors that Yasnaia
Poliana, too, was going to be destroyed, not by our own peasants but by others.

Tania told me afterward how they had packed everything
and awaited the pogrom from hour to hour. It probably would
have come, but the Yasnaia Poliana peasants had told the ri-
oters that they would meet them with pitchforks and axes. And
Tania had telegraphed to Kerensky, who immediately sent a
hundred soldiers to protect the estate. Now everything was
quiet.

The three ladies lived simply enough. The cook, Semen
Nikolayevich, had been dismissed. I met him in the village and
hardly recognized him. He was farming now. His once plump
red cheeks were unshaved and thin, his clothes rough, his big
round stomach was gone.

"I couldn't keep him any longer," mother said. "It was too
expensive."

But father's old valet, Ilya Vasilievich, was still serving dinner in his quiet way, though the food was scanty and his white
gloves were darned.

My mother was an old woman now. She sat dozing in a
rocking-chair all day.

"My eyes are very weak," she would say. "I can't write or
read any more."

She had some gold saved. She lived on that. I was astonished
to see how cool she was about everything that was going on
around her. Now that everything was lost, she did not worry at

all about her own welfare or the welfare of her children and grandchildren.

In the village, the peasants boasted that they had not even touched Yasnaia Poliana, but had defended the estate from their neighbors.

"It would have been a shame if you had," I said, sensing some regret under their words. "Didn't you get all the land of the estate free in 1911? What else do you want?"

"Sure," they agreed, "that's right. But in other places people got lots of things: furniture, clothes, cattle, machinery."

"And we never got anything," interrupted a woman nicknamed Queen Helen because she was the tallest woman in the village. "They got plenty from the landlords and what did we get? Absolutely nothing. It's not fair."

TOLSTOY'S SISTER

I RECEIVED a letter from Aunt Tania. She had been to see her sons in Petersburg and was going back to Yasnaia Poliana. She would stay with me a few hours in Moscow and wanted me to put her on the night train.

At that time, transportation had gone to pieces. Trains were irregular and very scarce. But crowds of people in the cities wanted to go to the southern grain provinces, where flour and bread could be got in exchange for clothes, shoes, tobacco, and soap. The railroads had been nationalized and certificates were being used instead of tickets. These were given to all workers and their families and were easy to get. But to put someone on the train was a different matter. Stations and platforms were packed with people who sat or lay on the ground, keeping an eye on their bags and boxes for fear of thieves. They would wait sometimes for days to get on a train, and when the train came in, it was rushed. The crowd stampeded, yelling and cursing. People were crushed and baggage smashed. Several times I saw the bodies of those who had been killed in the jam.

Once in such a *mêlée* someone seized my box and tried to get it away from me. I held on, but the crowd drove me along and nearly tore me in two. I fell on my back, still holding on to my luggage. Somebody's heel grazed my face. I shouted, and they picked me up.

People climbed through the windows and on to the roofs of the coaches, hung on the steps, or stood on the couplings. The police tried to drive them off, menacing them with the butts of their guns, but they kept pushing forward. Boxes and baskets burst open, women shrieked, windowpanes were broken.

I imagined my gentle old aunt in this scene. . . .

A cab took us to the station. The place was packed. The only train that was leaving that night for the south was "The

Maxim Gorky," a real proletarian train with nothing but fourth-class accommodations.

I singled out a porter with broad shoulders and told him to take the luggage. Leaving Aunt Tania seated in a corner of the station on one of her boxes, and, telling the porter to protect her from the crowd, I hurried to the station master.

"Comrade!" I said, "Tolstoy's sister is taking the next train and she's an old woman. She was Natasha Rostova in *War and Peace*. Please give her a seat in the train. She's going to Yasnaia Poliana."

The comrade blinked at me and gave no sign of understanding. If I had been talking of Karl Marx's sister, the result would have been exactly the same.

From all sides people were attacking him. "Comrade! Here is my certificate!"

"An urgent commission from the Commissariat!"

"Comrade, I insist on getting a seat in the train. I have government documents."

"I am a member of the party, comrade, from the Women's Department," shrieked a young girl. "I shall complain to the Central Committee, you are obliged . . ."

The station master jumped up, crossed the room, took down the telephone receiver, put it back again.

"Comrade, please, I beg you, the sister of Tolstoy . . ."

He drew in his head, hunched his shoulders, and walked out.

"He's gone out on the platform," one of the employees said. "No use waiting for him. He won't come back."

There was nothing to be done. We moved with the crowd toward the platform. I led the way and the huge porter guarded auntie from behind.

We were stopped in the passage.

"Is this your luggage? Open it."

"O Sasha, Sasha!" auntie cried. "They will mix up my manuscripts."

"Stop blocking the way! Move on!" There were shouts from the crowd behind us.

"Bourgeois! The devil take them! Don't you see the grandmother has just dropped down from the other world. . . ."

Auntie's hands were trembling. She could not find the keys in her handbag.

"What have you got here? Flour, bread?"

"Certainly not! Nothing of the kind!"

"Gold, that's what to look for. She's got gold and diamonds!"

"O Sasha, Sasha! How dreadful! They look like robbers!"

"Sh, sh, Auntie! For goodness' sake . . ."

The comrade shook out a few of auntie's dresses and blouses.

"All right. You can close your boxes."

We went out on the platform. The train had not yet come, but people were standing in a solid wall, pressing forward to get nearer the edge. At the end of the platform where the crowd was not so dense I seated auntie on a box, telling the porter to protect her. It was impossible to rush the train as everybody did, and even if we succeeded in pushing auntie in, she could not possibly stand with the mob in the train.

The train rumbled in, and before it stopped, the crowd surged forward and up the steps. Soldiers drove them off. There were curses, cries for help. Auntie sat on her box in her old-fashioned cloak and her little black fur hat, frightened and pitiful. The porter stood in front of her like a statue.

The scramble lasted a few minutes. Nearly everyone succeeded in squeezing on board, and only a few were left hopelessly trying to force their way in. I hunted up the chief conductor, whom I discovered I knew.

"Please help me," I begged. "My aunt, Tolstoy's sister, must get on your train. Please give her a seat."

The old man shook his head.

"I'd do it willingly," he said. "I've traveled with the dead count many times. But what can I do? There's no room."

"How about the employees' car?"

He waved his hand. "Full!"

The cars were buzzing like beehives. People were still trying to climb in.

I dashed along the train. All at once I saw a Pullman.

"Who is in this car?" I asked the porter.

"Commissars."

"Let me in. I want to speak to them."

"Impossible."

I went to the windows.

"Comrades! Comrades!"

No one answered.

"Comrades! Please come to the window. It's something urgent."

A disheveled head appeared.

"What's the matter, comrade?"

"The sister of Tolstoy, an old woman of seventy, simply must go to Yasnaia Poliana today. The crowd has nearly killed her—she is sick—please take her."

"And who are you?"

"Tolstoy's daughter."

"Wait a moment!"

The head disappeared and in a moment popped out again.

"We'll take your old lady."

I rushed to the other end of the platform where Aunt Tania was waiting.

"Auntie, Auntie! Come quickly!"

We ran to the Pullman. Auntie was gasping, and I was afraid she would have a heart attack. I pushed her into the car from below; the porter pulled her up.

Third bell. Whistle. The train started. Auntie was knocking at the window, smiling, and saying something that I could not hear.

In a few days, I got a letter from her. She had traveled very comfortably, the car had been warm and clean, and the comrades most cordial. "They even treated me to roast chicken," she wrote, "but they were disappointed that I was not Tolstoy's sister, but only his sister-in-law." "Now," she concluded, "I won't go anywhere, except to the other world."

V

THE TOLSTOY SOCIETY

TOWARD the end of 1918 a writer from Petersburg told me that some friends were thinking of publishing a complete edition of my father's works. In prerevolutionary days, many of his articles and pamphlets had been prohibited by the government, some of the novels, such as *Resurrection*, had been cut, and only a small proportion of the diaries and letters had been published. There was a great deal of unprinted material in the Rumiantsev Museum in Moscow—sketches, comedies, notebooks, diaries, letters, and many variants of *Childhood and Adolescence, War and Peace,* and other works. We estimated that a complete edition would consist of about ninety volumes. To prepare and publish them appeared impossible in this time of revolution. But the writer was optimistic. "We can start the editorial work at once," he said. "Then things may change. And we don't need much money to begin with."

The more I thought of it, the greater seemed the possibilities of the organization. So I went to Petersburg, where many of my father's friends—professors and members of the Academy of Science, and the famous lawyer and senator, A. F. Koni—were immediately interested. We worked out the regulations of the society and registered it. A group of us met almost every day at the home of a Finn who was a Tolstoyan to discuss the details of our new business. This Finn had been a sailor. His rooms looked like cabins and the walls were covered with pictures of the sea and yachts and ships. Around a great fireplace we used to discuss the problems of our organization.

I do not think that any of us were very businesslike, but we were enthusiastic. The sailor was perhaps the most practical; in any case he had his own methods. He never worried about money and never saved any, yet he had always earned it when he had to pay his bills. Many years before he had published father's prohibited articles. He had also smuggled our contraband literature in from abroad in his yacht. He looked more like a smuggler than anything else. His trousers were wide at the bottom, his cap was shabby, and he wore a short half-moon beard around his chin.

We called our organization "The Society for the Dissemination and Study of Tolstoy's Works." Of course we needed money. All our savings had been lost. Only the coöperative organizations were allowed to draw out their bank balances. Most of the money resulting from the publication of my father's posthumous works had been spent, as he had desired, in buying the land at Yasnaia Poliana and distributing it among the peasants. There were about twenty thousand rubles left. Vladimir Chertkov and I, as the executors of father's will, decided to use this money for the expenses of publication. With the help of the Coöperative Publishing House Zadruga, I succeeded in getting part of the money, and we started to work. Later on, Zadruga and two other coöperative organizations signed an agreement with our society to publish the complete edition and pay for the editorial work.

My father's manuscripts were preserved in two collections. His earliest writings up to 1884 had been collected by my mother and kept in the Rumiantsev Museum in Moscow; among them were *Childhood and Adolescence, The Cossacks, War and Peace,* and *Anna Karenina.* My mother used to tell how one of my brothers in cleaning out a closet once threw a bundle of papers out into a ditch. Happily mother found them before they were destroyed. They were the manuscripts of *War and Peace.*

After 1880, when father so completely changed his ideas and began writing books on religious and social questions, Chertkov took over the publication of his works, and father turned over to him all his manuscripts. Chertkov kept them in England until after the Revolution. Then he had them returned to Russia to the Tolstoy Museum in Moscow, where they are now.

We easily got permission to work on the manuscripts in the Rumiantsev Museum.

Our group consisted of a member of the Petersburg Academy of Science, two professors, my brother Sergius, two old-fashioned, aristocratic-looking ladies, two or three typists, and me. We worked all day in the museum wrapped in shubas, felt boots, fur hats, and gloves. Typing and writing in woolen gloves was not easy but as soon as we took them off our hands got cold and stiff. The museum was not heated; the pipes were frozen. The Bolsheviks did not worry about scholars who did not complain so long as they could continue to work in their beloved museum.

The chill in this big building, where the thick stone walls froze through and where the rays of the sun never penetrated, was worse than out-of-doors. One's feet were numb, and gradually the cold crept inside one. You felt as if your soul were congealing, you began to shiver all over, and the more you shivered, the more the cold crept into you. We tried to wrap ourselves tighter in our shubas, and to sit still, but we shook more and more.

At twelve o'clock, when we thought we could not stand the cold another minute, we were called to the basement. Big kettles of boiling water were brought from a restaurant. Each of us provided his own mug and a small package of food: a piece of bread, two boiled potatoes, some raw carrots. We tried to drink as much as we could—three or four cups—of something we called tea, but which was anything but tea: dried apples, carrots, herbs. It warmed us and gave us a feeling of satisfaction. We had half a day's work ahead of us.

Yet we were by no means disheartened. We were all absorbed in our work. Books were piled high on our tables. There were twelve boxes of manuscripts so tightly packed that many penciled notes were badly rubbed. Sometimes only two or three words out of a whole quotation would be legible. With the help of dictionaries we tried to make out the rest. There were several notebooks filled with folk expressions and proverbs, some of them not to be found in any dictionary. Evidently father had got them directly from the peasants. He had collected them before attempting to write his drama of peasant life, *The Power of Darkness.*

We forgot cold and hunger when we read over and over the variations of *War and Peace.* There were new and precious things in those dirty torn pages which my brother had thrown out into the weather, and we read them as if they were a current novel. New scenes, new episodes—we wondered sometimes why father had so pitilessly cut them out.

The ink on those manuscripts had faded. The handwriting was different, the letters were smaller and a little rounder. As he grew older, father's writing became larger and sharper, but it was always very difficult to read. Sometimes, after a whole day's work, we had deciphered only a few pages.

When my brother and I checked our copies of father's diaries with the original, we read the manuscript through five or six times, and each time found further mistakes that we had made in transcribing. It was exciting to puzzle out a sentence that had seemed to make no sense at all. We spent hours at that. In the *Diary* published by Chertkov the phrase "Plato's Symposium," seemed absurd in the context. It finally turned out to be "Newton's binomial theorem."

The aristocratic ladies copied and checked father's letters, written in French to his adored aunt, Tatiana Alexandrovna. Photographs were made of the unpublished manuscripts. We were afraid that the civil war, which was going on three hundred miles from Moscow and might easily come nearer, would result in the city's being shelled. So I sent the copies and photographs to different places; one of the copies went to Leland Stanford University in California.

We worked on the manuscripts for several years, and, all in all, those days in the cold hall of the Rumiantsev Museum were very bright against the gloomy times of the Revolution. The manuscripts are all catalogued and kept in good order now.

Later on, our society joined Chertkov's publishing organization. At that time all the coöperatives were either abolished or nationalized, and we no longer had money to continue the work. We decided to offer the results of our labor—Tolstoy's Complete Works—to the Government Publishing House, Gosizdat, for publication on the hundredth anniversary of his birth (1928). Our proposal was accepted, but only a few volumes out of the ninety have been published, and no one knows if the entire set will ever appear. The Soviet Government is not interested in spreading Tolstoy's ideas—it is printing an edition of only a thousand copies, at about three hundred rubles a set. But if the edition does not bring Tolstoy's ideas to the masses of the Russian people, the editorial work, which is still going on in Moscow, has, and will have in the future, a tremendous value. It is one of those heroic scholarly labors achieved by the Russian intelligentsia despite the conditions in which they have to live and work.

VI

A SECRET PRINTING-PRESS

I RENTED a lodging in Count Olsufiev's house. We had an office and library in the largest room. I lived in the other two small rooms.

Count Olsufiev, a former member of the Imperial Council, had fled abroad and now was declared an enemy of the people and sentenced to death. The house was nationalized, and the count's doorkeeper, Michael, was manager now. Michael had seemed to be devoted to the count, and everyone was astonished when he became one of the most ardent helpers and sympathizers of the Bolsheviks, denouncing people to whom not long ago he had opened the door with a flourish.

"You might tell me what you are looking for! I'd help you," I suggested with some temper to the agents of the Cheka who had been searching my lodging for more than an hour. They had opened nearly all the chests and cupboards, spilled out the dirty laundry, shaken my bedding, examined and knocked on the walls. "What is it? Guns? Proclamations? Jewelry?"

The men did not answer, but silently kept on searching. I was not worried. I had nothing forbidden—no guns, no gold. A few months before I had tied a string to my small revolver and let it down the chimney of the house next door. The only contraband I had was a piece of poetry, a satire on the Bolsheviks, but that I succeeded in sweeping off the table with my elbow, and a girl who lived in the same house and was working with us on father's manuscripts caught it and hid it in her dress.

I never got used to visits of this kind. They were utterly disgusting. Human dignity, self-respect, every right you have taken for granted all your life is violated, and you are helpless.

"Come here!" the Cheka leader said sharply. He reminded me of a corporal in the Tsar's army. And looking sideways at his companions, he pulled an order out from beneath a pile of papers and pointed at it.

"Search for a secret printing-press," I read with amazement.

"I can see now that there was nothing in it," said the Chekist. "You couldn't hide all the machinery."

"But where did you get such an idea?" I asked.

"It was reported to us that you were printing counterrevolutionary pamphlets here. The manager of this house . . ." he whispered.

"Do you know whose picture that is?" I asked, pointing to my father's photograph.

"No, I don't think I do. It isn't Karl Marx, is it?"

"No, it isn't. It's Lev Tolstoy, my father. He was a writer, and we are going to publish his works, but unfortunately they're not in print yet. We are only typing them."

"Oh, is that so?" he said thoughtfully. "Does the government know about it?"

"Certainly. Our society is registered."

"Hey, comrades!" the man called. "Come along! I don't think we'll find anything here!"

VII
BY FREIGHT

WHY are you shoving me?"

"I'm not shoving. My feet are tired. . . ."

"Stamping around like a mare! Not comfortable enough, eh? Lady, you'd better travel in a commissar's car if you don't like this one!"

"You poor pigeon!" a young woman whispered. "I guess you *are* tired. You're not used to it. Listen. Don't stand on your legs, just relax and lean on people; your legs will rest."

That was true. You could relax and hang on the shoulders of your neighbors. The train was so jammed that there was no danger of falling down. This trick enabled me to stand sometimes twenty or twenty-four hours on the way from Moscow to Yasnaia Poliana.

It was hard traveling in those cattle cars that were almost always packed, and the third- and fourth-class coaches were no better.

"Now where are you going, comrades?" people shouted from the cars, when the train stopped at a station and crowds tried to get in. "Don't you see how packed we are? There isn't room to breathe!"

"Don't let anybody in!" a woman cried. "They'll crush us to death! O lord! if I'd only known how terrible it would be!"

"You don't imagine that we're going to stay behind, do you?" men shouted from the platform. "Now, mother, make yourself thinner. Let's squeeze them a little and we'll get in all right!"

"Oh, oh! We'll be strangled! Hey, you! Don't you see that the car is full?"

One half of a man's body was in. He pushed with all his strength until he got his other foot in. But as soon as he was inside, his psychology changed:

"Move on, move on! This car's full!" he cried to those who

were trying to get on board. And again, no one listened to him. People kept on climbing into the car. Sometimes those inside shoved with all their might to keep others from getting in. If you happened to be in the middle of such a struggle, every bone and muscle in you was aware of it.

The cattle cars were never cleaned. Sometimes we had to stand in liquid manure. The trains went slowly, stopping at every station, no matter how small, and when the locomotive did not have enough fuel, it halted somewhere in the forest, and the passengers got out and chopped wood.

Once, when I was going to Moscow, I got into a cattle car that was not at all crowded. You could not only sit, but even lie down if you wanted to. The passengers were strange. Some of them were lying on the dirty floor and groaning. Others were talking excitedly as if they were delirious. Then I understood. They were sick with typhus, and were traveling from the south to Moscow, quite alone, without nurses or attendants. I wanted to get out, but when I thought of the difficulties of getting on another train, and when I pictured the crowded, filthy stations, I decided to stay where I was.

I did not mind traveling in a freight car, especially in summer. Sometimes it was even more comfortable than a passenger train.

MOONLIGHT. I was sitting in a coal car. The air was warm. My seat on the coal was comfortable. The only thing I was afraid of were the Bolshevik detachments that requisitioned provisions; they always caught people at the Laptevo station.

My neighbors seemed to be anxious, too. Some of them began to dig holes and hide their bags of flour under the coal. I didn't want to. I was very tired. Let come what would. The long train of coal cars rattled along until suddenly the cars began bumping and creaking and the train stopped.

"There they are! The detachment! By the third car!" people whispered. The soldiers came, wearing sharp pointed helmets, trailing their guns. Before we could move, they had reached us.

Silently and angrily they dug into the coal with their bayonets, hauling out sacks of grain and flour.

There were cries, men were lamenting in shrill women's voices. Sacks were thrown up in the air and fell heavily to the ground. Some people ran after the soldiers who were carrying the bags away.

"For Christ's sake, give me back my bread! I have a sick wife and five children in Serpukhov. I've been two weeks getting that bread. I'm worn out, hungry, full of lice. I thought at least my family wouldn't starve. . . ."

"Pigs, dogs, sons of the devil! They've ruined me," another was wailing. Then all at once, "You'll catch it! You will! Nobody can escape God's justice! Swine!"

"Shut up, if you don't want to go to prison!" a soldier growled.

I was sitting on my box. The other box and bag were lying beside me. The soldier began prodding the coal with his bayonet.

"There's nothing in there," I said.

"What have you got?"

"Flour, grain, potatoes, bacon."

"Going to sell them?"

"No, they're for myself."

"Oh, damn it!" and the Red soldier turned away. I was saved. There were no more requisitionary detachments until Moscow. In Moscow, at the central depot, baggage was inspected, but this train would not go that far.

I got several copies of *Izvestia* and spread them on the coal, put the sack of flour under my head, and fell asleep. When I awoke in the morning, I was as black as a chimney sweep. But I did not mind. We were in Moscow.

VIII

THE BENEFACTOR

THERE was hardly any life in the old Tolstoy home now. My mother and aunt—both old ladies—lived in the big house at Yasnaia Poliana, while my sister Tania and her little girl occupied the wing. Instead of the coming and going of visitors, instead of music, conversation, and the varied interests we had known, life was thoroughly dull. Sometimes auntie would try to break the tedium of the days by asking mother or Tania to accompany her singing, but it was not altogether pleasant to hear her sweet broken voice echoing in the old hall. There were too many memories for all of us.

I felt happier in the small house where the shadows of the past did not torment me and where little Tanichka was growing up—the joy and consolation of her mother and grandmother.

ONE night a troika stopped at the door. It was Prince Nikolai Obolensky,[1] who, with his wife and three children, was fleeing from his estate, which the peasants had been about to destroy. They had hardly had time to take the most necessary things with them. In one village through which they had passed, the peasants had stopped their horses and surrounded them. Anything might have happened if the coachman had not suddenly whipped up the team, so that the spirited animals bolted, knocking aside the men who were trying to hold them.

The Obolenskys stayed. Tania moved to the second floor, and later to the big house, leaving them the whole wing.

After a few months, Obolensky came to see me in Moscow. He told me that many people at Yasnaia Poliana, including my mother and sister, had suggested having the estate nationalized, first, because it would be safer to have it protected by the gov-

[1] The former husband of my sister Maria, who died in 1906.

ernment; and second, because my mother and Tania had no money to keep it going. The prince asked me if I had anything against his being manager. I said frankly that I did not believe in his capacities as a business man; but my opinion had no influence upon events, and he was appointed by the Commissariat of Agriculture.

In 1918 the Yasnaia Poliana Society was organized in Tula. It was composed of the intellectuals who were left in the city, and its aim was to protect the Tolstoy estate and to organize educational work for the peasants. It was just as well for the peasants, the local Communists and the Tula citizens to know that a society legally registered by the government was taking care of Yasnaia Poliana; and the mere fact of its existence at a time when the wave of peasant raids on estates was not yet over was very important. As for its educational work, that was mostly discussion.

One of the subjects most fervently debated in 1919 by the society was the offensive of the White army. Denikin was in the provinces of Orel and South Tula, about seventy miles from Yasnaia Poliana. A battle might easily take place at Yasnaia Poliana, which was situated on the highway between Tula and Orel. So it was decided to petition the staffs of both the Red and the White armies to avoid battle on Tolstoy's estate. The chairman of the society assured us that a telegram on the subject was sent to Denikin by the staff of the Red army.

The chairman played an important rôle at Yasnaia Poliana. He was a writer and had been acquainted with my father. He was tall and dark, with long arms and fingers, and he stooped as if he were too tall to stand erect. His voice was soft and his talk syrupy, he never spoke simply or intelligibly, and everything he did was mysterious. I seldom noticed his noiseless entrance into a room, but I often felt the uneasy weight of his presence before I saw him. Chekhov once said that he reminded him of a funeral hearse stood on end.

This man used to come to visit my father, always bringing some new invention. When automobiles were introduced into Russia he took my father for his first ride. Upon another occasion he brought as a present a gramaphone, and asked in return that father make records for it in four languages from his *Readings for Every Day*.

Now, as chairman of the Yasnaia Poliana Society, he occupied the library downstairs, which had been my father's study in the seventies. To the inhabitants of Yasnaia Poliana, he appeared as a savior. He was always distributing something: little pieces of soap, chocolate, buttons. He bestowed these trifles on people as if he were anointing them. With a shrewdness peculiar to him, he wheedled out of the government in the name of Tolstoy food, clothes, and other necessities for Yasnaia Poliana. But instead of storing them in the warehouse for fair distribution, he kept them, and from time to time made presents. Once, while I was at home, he distributed thirty pairs of boots among the employees of the farm and the household. I tried to find out where the boots came from and to whom they were really supposed to go. But the chairman was so vague and honeyed that I discovered nothing and only lost my temper. The next day a gang of men who were working on the road came to the house for the boots which the government had promised them. The chairman spoke to them suavely, reassured them, and promised that they should have their boots. A team of horses drove up to the front door early next morning, and in the afternoon a fresh supply of boots was distributed to the workers.

The idea of building a school in Tolstoy's memory first occurred to the members of the Yasnaia Poliana Society. They also planned to build a stone road between the estate and the highway, to repair the house and to reorganize the farm. The foundations of the school were laid, and lumber appeared in great quantities. Then one day the work stopped and the lumber disappeared. After a while another quantity of lumber was delivered, to be used for the repair of the house, I was told. Again nothing was done and the lumber disappeared; the chairman turned his attention to building the road. The prince, who had become interested in bees, began building out of fresh lumber a shed which he intended to use as an apiary.

Although the chairman no longer consulted anyone and acted independently, he still used the authority of the Tolstoy Society. Several times members of the society protested against such conduct on the part of the chairman of a collective organization. But he disarmed them with his torrent of words which confused the respectable gentlemen and made them feel as though they had intruded.

Never was the chairman's prestige among the inhabitants of Yasnaia Poliana greater than when, after having secured various certificates from the estate and the Society of Yasnaia Poliana, he started for the Ukraine to get food. There was a drought in 1919 in our district, and the government requisitioned all the grain, so that the peasants had nothing left to eat but potatoes. They baked bread out of acorns, green apples, and sorrel. There were great quantities of acorns that year, as if nature herself had taken care to save people from starvation. Men, women, children carried bags full from the woods. They were ground into flour and baked into bread that was tasteless and black but nourishing. The peasants had discolored teeth from eating it. It was always a little startling to see a handsome young girl or a child smile and show black teeth.

The chairman came back from the Ukraine with several carloads of flour, grain, and sugar, which were distributed to the workers on the estate and to the peasants roundabout.

"O dear Father!" the women exclaimed. "God send health and happiness to you and your children and grandchildren. You have saved us from death!"

A few days later the chairman said, "Tell the peasants that I need a hundred eggs. I am going to Moscow."

"For our benefactor!" said the women. "It's easy enough to get a hundred eggs for him! One egg from each house will make more than that!" And they brought him eggs and butter and homespun cloth.

"I don't know what we should do without him," the prince said. "I never saw a man like him. He can get anything he wants."

One day the chairman and the prince drove to Tula in two

sleighs, taking food with them for their friends and relatives. A detachment of soldiers was stationed on the road. They stopped Obolensky's sleigh.

"What have you got there?"

"Flour."

"You can't take it to town." And two men loaded the sacks on their backs and marched off with them.

"What have you got?" a soldier asked, looking into the sleigh in which the chairman was riding.

"Comrade!" the chairman interposed. "Comrade! Don't you realize that your life is precious to our government, our free country?"

The comrade opened his mouth.

"Dear comrade! You will catch cold. You shouldn't be so careless about your health. Come now, let me button your coat for you, like this!" And he began fastening the soldier's coat. "That's it! Thank you! You must not forget that the life of every soldier nowadays is precious to our revolutionary government!"

Bewildered, perhaps flattered, the soldier stood, while the "benefactor," patting the coachman on the back, said, "Go on, go on, we have lost sight of the first sleigh."

THE chairman became the sovereign of Yasnaia Poliana; he began to find fault with things and to be rude to my mother and sister.

"Why are you meddling in my business?" he would shout at my sister when she asked, for example, what he had bought. "Don't you know that your specific gravity is zero?"

My sister was hurt, but I was furious. I could not bear to go often to Yasnaia Poliana. Everything seemed too strange and hopeless, and there was little I could do to improve matters. My mother, sister, and aunt were not taken care of. Mother could get no one to help her wash the windows and put the winter frames in when it was getting cold. I remember her standing on the sill, cleaning the panes herself, with the windows open and the cold November wind blowing hard.

There were about a hundred and fifty people at Yasnaia Poliana receiving shares of food from the government, and hardly any work was being done. If an inspector had been sent there, he would undoubtedly have found a great deal wrong.

"The work in Yasnaia must go on like a splendid orchestra," the chairman said. "Everyone knows his own instrument and plays it, no false notes, no delays . . . ."

My sister listened with an ironic smile. She was used to such speeches. The prince smoked thoughtfully, elegantly holding a cigarette between his white fingers with their long polished nails.

My eldest brother, Sergius, who always took people very seriously, said, with that shyness that was strange in such a respectable-looking, bald-headed man:

"I should like to play one of the instruments in the orchestra."

"Pff!" sniffed the chairman. "Didn't I tell you that there was to be absolute harmony? You would undoubtedly bring in false notes. You might try the last violin."

I went to Moscow in the early part of 1919 and obtained an interview with Lunacharsky, Commissar of Education. He was very polite, rose as I entered, and shook hands with me.

"Sit down, I'm glad to see you. What can I do for you?"

At the first sound of his deep-toned, agreeable voice, I thought: "This man is kind," and, "He is an actor." Those first impressions never disappeared.

Two painters and a sculptor were working on portraits and a bust, and the commissar was posing. It seemed to me that everyone in the room, the commissar, the artists, the pale young secretary, the typists, the stenographers, every one of them was acting a part.

It was hard to talk casually in this atmosphere. I made my speech and concluded:

"I think that the Tolstoy estate ought to be not a Soviet farm but a museum, something like Goethe's home."

Before I had finished, the commissar jumped up and, never for a minute forgetting his rôle, began pacing the room and dictating to a stenographer. I watched him. Certainly this man with the pointed beard, gold spectacles, round stomach, and melodious voice was admiring himself and his power, and the boldness and quickness of his decisions. My amazement only added to his pleasure.

In a few minutes I was holding in my hands a paper which appointed me Commissar of Yasnaia Poliana, with all possible authority. At the bottom of the page was the signature of A. Lunacharsky in red ink, and the seal of the People's Commissariat of Education.

My victory was so easy that I did not even rejoice.

"Today I am a commissar, tomorrow I may be in prison," I thought to myself.

I dismissed the chairman. It was a hard and disagreeable job.

Later on I heard of him again. He evidently had not wanted to abandon a business somehow or other connected with the name of Tolstoy. He had procured certificates and started for the Ukraine. This time he had the brilliant idea of organizing a sanatorium for Ukrainian scientists in Gaspra, the former estate of Countess Panina in Crimea, where my father had been ill in 1901. He got hold of several wagons of food and bedding to start the sanatorium, but, on his way to Crimea, he changed his mind, and when he reached Sevastopol, sold everything and sailed off to Turkey. He told someone that he wanted to buy English clothes there. When the scientists came to the sanatorium in Gaspra, they found a cold, empty house and of course they had to go back.

Bulgakov, my father's former secretary, told me that when he was in Crimea he met the writer there, accompanied by an inspector of the Ukrainian Food Commissariat, the "Narkomprod." This inspector had been sent to investigate the matter of the sanatorium. The writer had already returned from Constantinople and must have done something with the English suits. He was now carried away by a new project: the organization of a Tolstoy Museum in Sevastopol. Instead of giving an account of his activities to the young official, he instructed him in the philosophy of Tolstoy. He spoke of his close relations with Tolstoy and the great meaning of Tolstoy's personality in his life.

I do not know how long this comedy lasted. I know that the writer avoided any kind of prosecution and that the Tolstoy family and the Tolstoyan organizations and societies were unanimous in disclaiming publicly all responsibility for his activities.

IX

"I REPENTED BITTERLY"

IN November, 1919, I had spent a few days in Yasnaia and was to start for Moscow at midnight. I packed my things and went upstairs to have tea. Auntie was sitting at a table playing a game of solitaire.

"Auntie dearest, tell me my fortune."

She finished her game, made me cut the cards with my left hand, and spread them out.

"That's bad!" she said, "very bad." And with a quick movement she swept the cards together.

"What was it, Auntie? Tell me, I'm not afraid."

"No, no. It was bad, I tell you. You can't always believe cards!"

But I kept at her: "Please, Auntie, I insist; tell me."

"All right, if I must, I'll tell you. Illness and death of a close relative. You won't go away tonight . . ."

For some reason I could not laugh and turn it into a joke. I felt sick at heart with the gloomy prophecy. The wind rattled the windowpanes, and the cold and darkness of out-of-doors seemed to enter the room.

"Auntie," I said, "if I cut the seven of spades,[1] you've really told me the truth."

The trees were rustling in the old park, the big-bellied samovar puffed and boiled on the tea table.

We were scarcely astonished when I turned up the seven of spades. A shudder ran down my back.

"And the ace of spades."[2]

And again we expected it. Now I was trembling from head to foot and auntie was pale.

"Nonsense! Are you mad?" auntie cried angrily, not know-

[1] The seven of spades means illness in fortune telling.
[2] Death.

ing herself what she was blaming me for. "Forget it and let's have tea. Go and call your mother."

With quick, light steps, she went to the table and began preparing the tea. I went to mother's room. A small kerosene lamp was burning dimly on her desk. Mother lay on the bed with her face turned toward the wall. She was crumpled in a heap and trembling from head to foot.

"What is the matter, Mama!"

"I am very cold, cover me up, will you?"

I covered her. Her head and neck were burning hot—I took her temperature. It was high. I undressed her and gave her some tea with wine. She was still shivering. Auntie and Tania came.

The doctors diagnosed pneumonia. Tania and I took care of her. She suffered a good deal. Her breathing was heavy and the cough suffocated her.

She did not complain, did not moan, was very patient and gentle.

One day she called Tania and me.

"I want to tell you, before I die," she said, "I was the cause of your father's death. He might have lived longer if I had not tormented him. I repented bitterly. But I never stopped loving him, and I was always a true wife to him."

Her large, dark, nearsighted eyes looked at us. They were very beautiful. Tania and I were both crying—she seemed so wonderfully calm, and I felt ashamed of the animosity I had once had for her.

The next day she was very much worse. She could not speak but her wide open eyes looked as though they knew us. I could not watch her suffering and left the room.

She was buried with Greek Orthodox rites in the cemetery beside my sister Masha.

X

EXCHANGE

TANIA and I were looking over the things in mother's old ironbound trunks. One enormous trunk was full of ikons that had belonged to our grandfather; in some were uniforms, in others mother's clothes. Tania pulled out an old-fashioned silk petticoat—that wouldn't do. Then mother's white cloak, trimmed with fur—she used to be very handsome in that, with her rosy, gentle face, and her hair parted in the middle in the old-fashioned way. No, not that, not for the world. A thick woolen coat—a jacket could be made out of it. You cannot get such good materials these days. We put that aside. A very large flannel dressing gown. That would do. And a piece of serge. I was sorry to let that go, but there was nothing to be done. That would buy forty pounds of flour at least, maybe more.

My nephew Ilya and I put the bundle of clothes into the bottom of a sleigh. Ilya was a tall slender boy of seventeen. He wore his father's white Russian coat with a belt around his waist and a high gray fur hat. The big-headed bay stallion drew the light sleigh along as easily as a plaything. Ilya sat sideways, as all good coachmen do, with his right foot sticking out in case the sleigh should swerve.

It was about thirteen miles to the village called "Cows' Tails." We stopped at the house where father used to rest on his way to his brother Sergius' estate. The owner of the house led our stallion through the broad door of the barn, unbridled the animal, and gave him a whole armful of hay.

The house was large but it had only two rooms. The first was the so-called "dirty room," which contained a stove and a large bed of boards; the second the "clean room," with geraniums on the window sills, a creeper hanging from the ceiling, and on the walls a few fashion plates and pictures of generals from the magazine *Niva*.

The samovar was set on the table and there were ham, bacon, black bread, and honey. These peasants were well off. Their land was fertile, their crops good, and they had plenty of wheat, millet, and rye. They could not buy any clothes, but people came from the city to exchange shoes, rubbers, soap, tobacco, and clothes for flour and grain.

I undid my bundle. The women examined the clothes attentively, not missing the smallest stain or hole in an old petticoat. They spread the cloth against the window, rubbed it with their fingers, and tried the material with their teeth.

"No more than five pounds of rye for this petticoat."

I felt very uncomfortable, but I bargained. I wanted ten. At last we agreed on six and a half pounds.

"I want to ask you," said an old woman who had taken no part in the bargaining, but had sat silently in a corner, "I don't understand why, after being so rich, having such a great big estate, you are exchanging old rags for bread. Where have all your riches gone to? What have they done with all the belongings of the count? If I were you, I'd just order them: 'Bring me so many pounds of wheat and rye and buckwheat from the storehouse.'"

"Impossible, Grandmother!" I answered. "Everything belongs to the government now. If I order grain, or if I take it myself, they'll put me in prison."

"I don't understand it. How can that be? What right have they got to take what belongs to you? How can you go on living, if everything is taken away? Listen, little daughters," she suddenly addressed the young women, "don't bargain too much. Just add a pound or two to the bargain. If the masters did not need food so badly, do you think they would have come and offered us all these old clothes of theirs?"

"That's true, Grandmother," I said, "I hate doing it. But I am going to Moscow now and people cannot buy any food there."

"Never mind, never mind. You have to forget your pride now. I remember when you or your sisters would ride on horseback to your uncle's—on horses, real lions!—and you ladies perched on one side. I always wondered why you didn't tumble off. You would stop here and we would set the samovar and everything we had on the table. You would tip us, and sometimes you hadn't any change in your pockets and you would give us a gold piece. And I would bow and say, 'Thank you, Your Excellency. I wish good health to Your Excellency.' Everything changes in this world."

We were very jolly when we drove home. The moon was shining; the wide plains spread before us. Here and there shone the little yellow lights of peasant huts. There was no one outdoors and the only sound was the creaking of the runners on the snow. Bags full of flour and grain lay at the bottom of the sleigh. Now and then I felt with my foot the heavy piece of bacon wrapped up in newspaper, to be sure we did not lose it.

"If only I can get all this food to Moscow," I thought, "I'll have nearly enough for the whole winter."

XI

THE COLONEL'S WIFE

MIDNIGHT. The room was very cold. The furnace had not run for more than a year and the "Lilliputian," as we called the small iron stove, had filled the room with smoke so that I had to put it out. It took courage to wash oneself for the night; the temperature in the bathroom was not more than one or two degrees above freezing.

In bed at last under a pile of woolen and cotton blankets and a fur coat. A blessed warmth crept through my body. But my feet were as cold as ice. I drew my hand out from under the covers, put out the light and fell asleep.

Bang! Bang!

I woke up in a panic. The door was shaking with blows. The bell, of course, was out of order, like every other apartment bell in Moscow.

"Hey, there! Are you deaf? Open the door."

The blessed warmth left me quickly. I began to shiver, perhaps with cold, perhaps with fright.

"Well, are you going to let us in? It is the president of the house committee."[1]

"Wait a moment."

My bare feet found my felt boots. I tried to pull on my dressing gown. One of the sleeves had turned inside out and would not go on.

"Damn you!" I did not know what I was cursing—the cold, the sleeve, or the man who was knocking at the door.

"What do you want? It's midnight."

"We must search you."

The president of the house committee, with turned-up collar, stepped in, shrugging his shoulders. Then the small antechamber filled with "leather coats."[2]

[1] A managing committee chosen by the residents of the apartment house.
[2] The nickname for the Secret Police.

"Have you a search warrant?" I asked.

"Yes," answered the president, avoiding my eyes. He had an order not only for a thorough search but for my arrest.

In a few minutes I was standing in a dark, lonely street with my hastily packed bag. There was silence all around—no one was in sight. The "leather coats" were busy with their motor car. And suddenly the machine began to roar, resounding between the walls.

"Get in quickly."

A mad idea flashed through my head. "What if I try to run away?" A feeling of terror came over me, the feeling I had in the war during a cannonade. I could hear my teeth chattering. But running away was as impossible now as it had been at the front.

As the machine rushed through the empty streets of Moscow toward the prison of the Secret Police, I began to grow calmer. I do not know what quieted me—the speed of the machine or that nameless feeling that protects one from fear of hunger, imprisonment, or death. But there was no longer any fear in me when we reached the prison.

They put me in a cell. The lock clicked. I found a pallet in the dark, lay down, and fell asleep. It seemed to me that I had slept but a short while when a guard called:

"Hallo, citizens! Get up. Tea is ready."

I opened my eyes. It was dark in the cell. The wall of the neighboring house shut off the light. A fat elderly woman was sitting on the pallet next to me and hunting for something in a large basket. Her efforts seemed to get her quite out of breath. In another corner three fair-haired, blue-eyed girls, all very alike, were talking gaily together.

"Latvians," the fat woman whispered. "They're in prison for speculating in jewelry."

"Why are you here?" I asked.

She looked at me suspiciously.

"I? Well—I really don't know. It's a long story."

I saw that she was afraid of me. But she was also talkative and bursting to tell her troubles to somebody. In a short time I heard her whole history. At first she kept looking at the Latvian girls and tried to speak in a whisper, but as they paid no attention to her she went on with her story and forgot them.

Her husband had been a colonel in the old Russian army. Then he had fled with the White army to the south. She lived with her stepdaughter and her son, a boy of fifteen, in Moscow. They were very poor. She had had to sell anything she could to get food.

For a long time she had not known whether her husband was alive or dead. But a month ago a soldier had come from the White army and brought her a message from him. He was well; he had not forgotten his family; he hoped that things would change for the better, and that he would soon be with them.

"Oh, I nearly went mad I was so happy," she told me. "I could not do enough to entertain him. I heated the samovar and lighted the stove. I had some white flour and fresh butter. I baked him cakes. I got some lump sugar that I had saved in my trunk. I gave him jam for tea. Oh, I treated him as well as I could. And he—he told me all about my husband—how he looked, how he lived, and how he spoke about us. You cannot imagine how upset I was! And I said:

"'O God! When shall we be able to live together? When will all our sufferings be over?'

"'Very soon,' the soldier said, 'very soon. The White army will come to Moscow and then all your troubles will be finished.'

"And I sighed and said, 'O God be merciful to us sinful creatures. Put an end to our sufferings.' Believe me, that's all I said, nothing else. Nicholas and Annie were sitting there, listening. Nicholas is such a sensitive boy he began crying.

"Well, about six in the evening we saw the man off, and we didn't bother with supper; only Nicholas ate some porridge. We were too excited. Nicholas couldn't learn his lessons. He kept talking about his father. About eleven I put the children to bed and lay down myself. But I couldn't sleep. I was so happy and so restless.

"Then I heard the noise of a car under the windows. We live on the other side of the Moscow River, in a very quiet little street. Automobiles don't come there much. But—I heard distinctly, there could be no mistake—the car stopped right in front of our house. I held my breath, my heart sank.

"Officers rushed in. Three of them. They searched the house. Of course they didn't find anything. They took Nicholas and me; they put us in the car and brought us here. Nicholas was as pale as death, but he tried to soothe me. 'Don't be afraid, Mother,' he said, 'it's a misunderstanding. They'll let us out soon.' But I knew right away that the soldier was a spy. Nicholas is in a cell above us."

And covering her face with her puffy hands, the woman cried bitterly.

"I'm not afraid for myself," she went on. "I'm afraid for Nicholas. He's just a child, just a child." And again her fat body shook with sobs. "Oh, why did they take us, even if this man was a spy? I didn't say anything, nothing at all." Then leaning her heavy body toward me, she whispered in my ear: "They'll shoot me. I know it. I feel they will. O Nicholas! My boy! What will become of him? He'll be lost without me."

And she cried again. I tried my best to comfort her.

The next morning the guard brought her some sugar wrapped in a piece of newspaper.

"The young citizen in the upper cell sent that to you," he said.

"Nicholas, my darling!" exclaimed the woman. "No, no, I don't want it. He shan't give up his sugar. He's sent me all his day's ration. For heaven's sake, take the sugar back; tell him I have plenty."

She got her plump legs off the pallet; but when she reached the door the guard was gone, and she was left standing there, reaching out her hand with the sugar.

In the morning the Latvian girls were set free, and I was called for questioning. When I came back the colonel's wife wanted to know what the examining magistrate had asked me.

I did not care to speak about myself; and the woman was so eager to discuss her own affairs that she soon stopped questioning me, and talked about Nicholas and his kind heart, and over and over said that the Reds would kill her.

The next day the guard came in again with a broad smile and brought the mother a day's ration of sugar and a piece of herring from her son.

"I never saw such a boy in my life!" she sighed. "Never! And what if he is . . . if they . . . Tell me—they can't kill a child, can they? He is only fifteen, just a boy, a child."

She talked so wildly that I had no time to think about myself. I did everything I could to calm her, but she cried all day long and did not sleep at night.

On the fifth day of my arrest the guard came to the cell.

"Citizen Tolstoy," he said, "get your things ready."

"Where are you taking me?"

"Home."

I began to pack as fast as I could. The colonel's wife bustled around me and seemed much more excited than I was. When I was ready to go, the guard moved to the door. At this moment the woman slipped something hard into my hand.

"Give that to Nicholas, to the children, when I am dead," she whispered. "That is all I have. Here is the address," and she stuck a piece of paper in my pocket.

"Hurry up," the guard cried. Picking up my bag, I followed him.

"Leave the bag here," he said when we reached the office.

"Where are you taking me?"

"To the magistrate."

I took out my pocket handkerchief, wrapped the hard objects that the colonel's wife had given me in it, and held them tightly in my hand.

"If they find them, I'll be executed," I thought.

The magistrate's questioning was a mere formality. He had no proofs whatever of my counterrevolutionary work, and an order was given to set me free. I was taken back to the office.

The agents of the Secret Police had opened my bag, and were searching it. They led me into a small room where a Latvian girl met me.

"Undress. I must search you."

I took off my dress.

"Don't you understand?" she cried. "Take off everything."

Now only my shirt, stockings, and shoes were left.

"Damn you!" she shrieked. "Don't you hear what I say? Take off everything."

I stood naked in front of the girl, gritting my teeth and clenching my fists with rage, and wiping the perspiration from my forehead with the handkerchief in which the hard objects were wrapped.

"What does this mean?" exclaimed the girl in a piercing voice, as she drew out of my pocket the scrap of paper with the address of the fat woman.

I dressed, and, as if scalded, rushed out of the prison and ran until I got home. Only then did I unfold the handkerchief. It was full of precious stones—a ring with nine diamonds, earrings with seven big diamonds. The things were old fashioned and showy, but they were certainly valuable.

What was to be done? The address was gone. It was dangerous to keep precious things. Jewels had been declared nationalized by the government, and people were put in prison or executed for keeping them.

A dying plant stood on the window sill. I dumped the earth out of the pot, wrapped the jewels in an old oilcloth, put them in the bottom, and again planted the flower.

"When the colonel's wife gets out of prison she will come for them," I thought.

But she did not come. I heard nothing of her for two years. The pot with the dead flower stood on the shelf in the kitchen. Every time I looked at it I thought of the round, naïve face of the woman.

"Where is she?" I wondered. "Why doesn't she come for her jewelry?"

Thinking of her made me depressed and I tried to put her

out of my mind. I had other things to think about, too. One had to struggle desperately to live, to get food, wood, clothes, for there was nothing to be had at the stores. Rumors spread through Moscow: "The Bolsheviks are searching for arms." And the people of Moscow tried to get rid of old hunting guns, Finnish knives, and anything that might be looked on as a dangerous weapon. They were afraid to give them up to the Soviet, as they were ordered to do. There would be questions: "Where did you get this gun? Why did you keep it so long?"

"The Bolsheviks are searching for gold and jewelry." And again there was panic. I was terribly worried about the jewels intrusted to me by the colonel's wife. What if the Secret Police should take them away? What should I tell her?

Then for a while I forgot all about her.

XII

CITY LIFE

THEY say that the best way to teach a man to skate is to lead him to the middle of a lake and leave him, and the best way to teach him to swim is to throw him into the water. Something like the latter happened to the Russians. They were plunged into an ocean of trials; some drowned, some swam.

People who had never been near a stove learned to cook; they learned to do washing, to sweep streets; they had to hunt for food, sell, exchange, travel on the roofs of trains, on the couplings. They even learned to steal. But what was to be done?

On the one hand, trade and transportation were chaotic. The government could not supply the people with food, clothes, and fuel. The small amount allowed on the food cards was certainly not enough to live on: one-half pound of bread a day, a pound of oil every month, once in a while a herring or a few pounds of cereal. On the other hand, the government arrested all those who brought supplies into the cities—among them the so-called "bag men," who smuggled food into Moscow and exchanged it for clothes and things needed in the country. Money was worth nothing.

I lived like everyone else, scraping up just enough to get along, and I managed to have my dinner every day—cereal and carrot or cabbage soup, with plenty of salt, but no butter or meat. I ate a lot and felt full after the meal, but not satisfied. I had no kerosene and very little wood with which to cook. Someone told me how to wrap the soup kettle in paper, cover it with pillows and warm clothes and let the soup cook. I tried that several times but never succeeded in making it work. Then I heard of a magic little box in which food was cooked without any fuel. I got one. You had to put your well-covered pans with boiling food into the wooden box, which had double sides, filled in between with shavings. In about two or three hours, the food would be done. This fireless cooker was very useful to me. A peasant girl who sometimes helped me was much interested in the arrangement.

"I don't believe you can cook without fire," she said. "People just invent God-knows-what, and only confuse our poor brains."

I explained how she was to cook the dinner, and went to the museum. I was very hungry when I came back but the meal was not ready.

"I told you," the girl said, "it's crazy. You can see everything's raw."

"But I cook my dinner every day! It is always ready and hot. Now tell me how you did it."

The girl confessed that she was so interested in the cooker that she kept opening the lid and looking into it to see how it could possibly cook without fire. She had of course let all the steam out.

One of my friends, the writer Khiriakov, used to come often to eat with me. He was always hungry. His big head was curiously stuck on a scrawny neck, and his old-fashioned waistcoat, hanging loosely on his body, could not hide the terrible protruding bones. The scanty lunch he brought with him to the museum was only a morsel. He needed ten times as much to fill his great empty skeleton.

"Are you satisfied sometimes?" I asked him.

"No, never."

And I decided to feed him as much as he could possibly eat. I made him enough cereal to last me at least four days.

"Please help yourself!"

He ate and ate, pouring soup over the cereal to make it softer. He ate slowly, enjoying his meal as a man does who knows the value of food. And when there was nothing left:

"Have you had enough?" I asked.

"Well, I don't know, I think I could eat some more."

You had to have wood to heat your little stove once a day to boil your dinner and warm yourself. Sometimes you could buy a bundle of wood in the streets, but it was very expensive; millions, billions of rubles—I don't remember how much, for at that time money was so cheap that you paid a hundred rubles for a box of matches.

At first wood was everywhere. Moscow was wrecked for firewood. The first to go were the old wooden houses and fences. In the side street where I lived, two houses were demolished; on the Nikitskaya a little farther on they were tearing down a fence.

For a time no one guarded the ruins and everybody dragged away beams and boards, hauling them on sledges or carrying them on their backs. People stored wood in the kitchens of their lodgings or hid it under their beds. I knew a man who half filled his room with wood. Later on the ruins were guarded.

It is night. A Red soldier is walking up and down, trying to warm himself near a fire.

"Comrade, may we take a log of wood?"

"Move on, move on, comrades!"

"Let us have a small log of wood. We are freezing to death!"

"Move on, I tell you, or I'll have to take you to the police station!"

"Can't we make a bargain? We'll bring you tobacco and a pot of hot potatoes for some wood!"

For a moment the soldier is silent; then he yields.

"All right, but hurry up. I'm going to be relieved."

We run to the house and hurry back with the potatoes and tobacco. A girl who works at the museum and lives on the first floor of my house is with me. We choose the biggest beam we can find and load it on our shoulders. It is very heavy and so long that we cannot carry it up the stairs. We push it through the window on the ground floor and half of it sticks out into the street. Never mind. We can't lose any time. We run back to the wreckage. The Red soldier has finished his supper and is smoking a cigarette.

"Comrade, may we take another?"

He is satisfied and in a good humor: "All right, I'm not watching you."

A second beam sticks out of the window. We saw the beams in half and push them into the room. We have wood for at least two weeks.

Sometimes there are no guards in sight but there are figures in the dark near the half-demolished fence. They may be guards, one can't tell in the dark. I hide my ax under my leather jacket. Those people are undoubtedly watching me. I do not dare to go nearer. For some time we observe each other. Then I go off and hide behind a neighboring house.

Crack, crack! They are tearing down the fence.

"Camels!" I exclaim joyfully and hurry to pull the fence down from the opposite side.

The silhouettes of the people loaded with wood really look like camels.

EVERYTHING stopped working in the first years of the Revolution. Telephones, heating systems, nothing mechanical was in order; street cars did not run. I rode wherever I had to go on my bicycle, carried food home on it from the railroad station, and sometimes even wood. In the summer, I rode into the country. I became really fond of the bicycle and took good care of it: there were no new ones to be bought. And then I heard that all bicycles were to be requisitioned by the government.

The girl from the first floor also had a bicycle, which she had got in exchange for a sewing machine. She was as worried as I. We could not hide them in our small lodgings and it was impossible to ship them anywhere. They would simply be confiscated at the railroad station.

One Saturday—a warm, rainy summer day—we put three cans of meat and some boiled eggs in our knapsacks. The wind blew against our backs and before us was the white stone highway. We sped off. The bicycles ran with surprising ease and we made the one-hundred-and-thirty-mile trip to Yasnaia Poliana in forty-eight hours, left our bicycles there, and returned to Moscow by train.

SOMETIMES I had to sell things in the Smolensky market. The merchandise lay spread out on the sidewalk: old shoes, a clock, a necklace, a teapot, lace, old dresses. I would sit at the edge of the pavement, watching the passers-by, hearing people talking French, exchanging greetings with old acquaintances—there were many of them here. All sorts of people pushed up, handled my things, bargained and joked.

"How much for the necklace? What? Five lemons?[1] One lemon is plenty!"

"If you can give me flour or bacon," I suggested meekly, "I'll make it cheaper, but for money—no."

It was hot, dust got into one's pores . . .

"Little madam! How much for the teapot?" a fat woman asked.

I was tired out and sold the teapot for half the price. At the same market I bought food, loaded the remaining things on my back, and walked home.

ONCE in a while the Tolstoyan sailor would come from Petersburg. He took photographs of father's manuscripts and stayed in the office of our society, in the house where I lived.

"Are you busy today?" he asked me once when we were having dinner.

"No, what do you want me to do?"

"Let's go to the commissariat."

"What for?"

"To sign our names, that's all."

"What do you mean?"

"Oh, well, we'll marry, and you will be a citizen of Finland. You will be absolutely free, you can go abroad if you like with a passport, the Finnish Consulate will protect you, and nothing will change in our lives."

[1] Millions were called lemons.

I hesitated.

"No, it's awfully nice of you but I guess not. What if you fall in love and want to marry for good?"

He tried to persuade me, but I was stubborn.

Life was strange in those times!

XIII

SPRING

IN winter everyone walked in the street in Moscow. It was impossible to use the sidewalks; they were all ice. Under the drain pipes, where the water froze in sheets, it was especially slippery, and your feet without rubbers (for rubbers had disappeared from the shops as mysteriously as had everything else) slipped at every step.

People usually took bags or small sledges with them, in case they had a chance to buy something—butter, a piece of horse meat, or a herring. I remember seeing a lady with a shabby astrakhan coat and muff, remnants of her former wealth, dragging along a small sled which jerked from side to side, skidding and hitting passers-by.

One day in March I felt as cattle must feel in the early spring, when their winter supply of food is giving out and they get very thin and scrawny and unsteady on their legs. There was a horrid emptiness in my head, I felt sick; my body was unnaturally light and I shivered continually with the cold.

"It's too bad that we haven't fur," a seventy-five-year-old princess once said to me. To keep warm, she burned a kerosene lamp which smoked dreadfully. The gray-headed princess got darker every day. Her hands and face were covered with soot.

In the publishing house Zadruga, everybody talked of the latest arrests. I was tired of these conversations. Every day it was the same thing: searches and arrests; today my neighbor is arrested, tomorrow they will arrest me. It is as inevitable as cold, as hunger.

Wood was being distributed in the yard. Dry birch wood, quantities of it. It would all be taken away on sleds by the employees of Zadruga: writers, professors, scientists, typists.

"We must hurry," said a thin typist who was dragging a tiny sled. "The road will soon be spoiled!"

"Can you manage that load?" asked the janitor.

"Oh, I won't take it all at once. I'll come several times. Please, will you give me my share?"

"Where do you want me to put it? Don't you see how stacked the yard is?"

"Oh, please, I'll take it as soon as I can. I don't live far away. How much will I get?"

"One eighth. And what a sled you've got! It will break if you put one good log on it.

A girl who worked with me in the Tolstoy Society came along to help me get my share. We brought large sleds, loaded them as heavily as possible, and tied the wood with ropes. The dirty gray snow crunched heavily under the runners. There was not much left and the runners grated on stones. I dragged my load with difficulty. My heart was pounding and my legs trembled. I felt sick again. The thought of some cocoa-butter cookies I had at home only made me feel worse.

We moved slowly, stopping often to rest. My leather jacket was open and I was steaming like a tired horse.

"This damned life!"

I longed to sit down there in the dirty snow and weep.

Some children were playing in the street, shouting and laughing as if they felt the coming of spring. A plump little chap with green mittens caught hold of my sled.

"Let go!" I cried angrily. "It's heavy enough without you!"

But he did not let go. Holding on to the rope, he ran by my side. The rest of the children followed.

A girl of about six in a dirty white hood came running up.

"We'll help you!" she cried, and turning to the others, said indignantly:

"Well? What's the matter with you?"

The children hesitated; then they made a rush for the sleds.

"Now, all together!"

The sleds sped away. Some of the children pushed from behind, some from the sides, several pulled. The rope that had been hurting my shoulders a few minutes before loosened. I had to walk faster, almost run.

There was a ditch across the road. "Slower, slower!" the

white hood called. "Be careful!" Her cheeks were flushed, her black eyes sparkled beneath the white wool. The children did not listen. They were too excited.

"It's all right!" green mittens shouted. "Here she goes!" The rope on my shoulders went slack, the sled jerked and bumped at the edge of the rut. There was a splash. The load was in the water.

The children surrounded the sled. For a moment there was absolute silence. Like a grown-up person, the girl in the white hood thrust her little hands apart.

"Well, I never!"

"What's the use of standing like that and wasting time?" a boy who seemed older than the others cried. "One, two, three!"

"Mishka, you devil, you stepped on my foot," someone squeaked.

"Never mind. It'll be all right before your wedding."

Before I could get hold of the edge of the sled there was another splash and the load was straightened out. One more effort and the sled came out of the rut. The second sled was taken past with the greatest care.

The road ran into the Bolshaia Nikitskaia, which went up-hill.

"Children!" I said, "go home, you'll get lost."

"What an idea!" sniffed the white hood disdainfully. And gripping the rope with her tiny hand, she kept on marching beside me. "What an idea! I go to kindergarten every day all alone."

"And I go shopping!"

"And I know where my aunt lives!"

"We'll deliver the wood for you!" the oldest boy said.

"And unload it, too!" green mittens added.

"Yes, of course we'll unload it for you!" said the white hood.

They pulled the sleds up the hill as easily as if they were playing a game. Then they helped me unload the wood and store it. When we had finished, sitting on the logs, the children ate my cocoa-butter cookies. I watched. I was no longer sick with hunger. I was happy. I felt the spring.

XIV

I HEATED THE SAMOVAR

ONE day toward the end of March, 1920, I was returning to Moscow from Yasnaia Poliana. Again I had to travel in a cattle car and stand for more than twenty hours. My feet ached dreadfully, my eyes were swollen, and I felt lice creeping all over my body. I longed for a bath, a cup of hot tea, and a warm bed, and I wondered whether I had the strength to get home and carry my things upstairs. How frequent that feeling was: I have no strength left, I am utterly exhausted, my feet will not hold me; but I must go on, one more effort, another . . . There is a limit to patience and strength, but it seems to advance with difficulties. One gets used to suffering and learns how to bear it.

There was the seal of the Secret Police on my door. What could that mean?

I left my things at a neighbor's and ran to the telephone.

"Kremlin . . . The Secretary of the Central Executive Committee! The Commissar of Yasnaia Poliana is speaking."

I knew the secretary and as soon as I got hold of him, began telling him indignantly that I had just come from Yasnaia Poliana, that I was very tired, and that I wanted him to order the police to let me into my room. I was certain that there was a misunderstanding. I had not meddled in politics. I had no arms, no gold or anything prohibited at that time by the government.

In about ten minutes the secretary called me back: "The agents of the Secret Police will be there in a few minutes. They say that the matter is serious."

The curt tone of the secretary, who was usually very polite, surprised me.

Two uniformed agents of the Cheka came. I did not quite understand the rôle of a very slender young man dressed in a velvet blouse, with a pale, unhealthy face, languid eyes, and long curly chestnut hair, who accompanied them. There was something abnormal and strange in his whole appearance.

"You . . . ?"

"I am with them," he nodded at the agents. "I am an artist, a futurist."

"And a Chekist?"

"Yes, I am an agent of the Cheka."

They did not search long, and they found nothing.

"Pack up," one of the agents said.

"Why?"

"You are arrested!"

"Arrested? What for? You didn't find anything."

"There is an order to arrest you."

"Impossible!" I cried. "Absolutely impossible! Why? I am the Commissar of Yasnaia Poliana! I have had nothing to do with politics! This is a misunderstanding!"

"Please get your things."

"Indeed I won't, I tell you! This is absurd!"

My indignation and protests were so earnest that the police, leaving me in the care of the artist, went to the neighboring house to telephone to the Cheka.

Yes, they had an order to arrest me immediately.

"But I have money and accounts belonging to the government. I must put them in order. Give me three hours or I won't go."

And again the Chekists went to the telephone.

"All right," they said when they came back, "but be quick about it."

My niece and some friends who had come to welcome me had the samovar ready in a moment. The artist helped himself to tea and the provisions I had just brought: white bread, honey, butter, jam.

I took a bath, changed my clothes, packed, and gave my accounts and money to my niece. We got to the Lubianka prison about nine o'clock in the evening. I was kept in the office of the commandant until one. The commandant, a big man with sandy hair and a perpetual malignant smile, took away my scissors, penknife, and needles. Sitting on a chair I fell asleep.

At one o'clock I was questioned by the examining magistrate.

"Do you remember having meetings in your rooms?" he asked.

"No, I don't," I answered, suddenly understanding why I had been arrested.

More than a year before, some friends had asked me to lend them the office of the society for a meeting. I consented. I had known that the meeting was a political one, but at that time I had never suspected that it was a gathering of the so-called Tactical Center that was planning the Whites' advance on Moscow under General Denikin. I did not take part in the meetings, although once or twice I heated the samovar and served tea. Sometimes there was a telephone call for me, but when I entered the room to answer it, everyone was silent. I had forgotten all about those meetings. Now, for the first time, I realized that my situation was serious.

XV

RATS

"COMRADE," I said to the guard who led me to a cell, "won't you give me a mug of water?"

"No, there's no rule for giving water to prisoners at night . . ."

He shut the door, and the lock clicked in the stillness.

I looked about me. The cell was very small. Along one wall was a wooden pallet made of three boards very badly stuck together. There was a plain chair, and nothing else in the room. I hardly had time to spread my plaid over the boards of my cot and get a pillow from my bag before the light was turned off and I was left in the dark.

When I was younger I had a happy gift. After strong emotion, suffering, strain of mind and will, there was always a beneficent reaction. I could fall asleep wherever I was, in any position, lying or sitting. During the war I even succeeded in sleeping on horseback. Now I thought I should fall asleep immediately. I closed my eyes, but instantly opened them and began listening. There was a rustle in the heating pipes. It grew louder and louder; I sat up and listened. There seemed to be living creatures in the cell. Something fell softly on the floor. Once, twice, three times. Now I could hear distinctly. The room was full of rats, lots of them running about the floor, scraping against the walls. I knocked at the edge of the bed to frighten them. For a moment the noise ceased but then it began again. The room was alive. I could hear rats scratching and squeaking in every corner. I knocked again. Now they paid no attention. I was the intruder, they were the masters here, and they became more and more impudent as time went on.

"I hope they won't creep into my bed," I thought. And at that very moment I could feel them climbing up on to my plaid, on to my legs.

Wet with perspiration, I shook the edge of the plaid. Two or three animals fell to the ground with a plop. I tucked the cover up, so that they could not reach me. That did not help. They crawled up the wall, up the legs of the pallet, on to the window sill, I could feel them. . . .

I seized the chair, and began hitting about in the darkness. Again I heard the animals squeaking and scampering.

"Hallo, citizen! Do you want to be thrown into solitary?" cried the guard, looking into the cell. "What are you making all this noise for?"

"Please turn the light on," I begged. "The cell is full of rats."

"It's against the rule," he said and walked away.

There was silence for a few moments. My eyes closed. I was so tired. Then I heard the rustling again near the heating pipes. And in a few moments the creatures filled the room. They swarmed on me from every side. Nearly crazy with horror, I rushed to the door and shook it with all my strength. It did not move.

Suddenly it came over me that I was locked in with these terrible creatures. I could not get out. I could not do anything. Tears of helplessness came to my eyes. I jumped on my pallet, threw myself on my knees, and beat the wall with my head. The noise kept the animals from crawling on to my bed. As time passed the strokes of my head against the wall became slower. My eyes closed.

"Our Father, which art in Heaven," I said, knocking at the wall, "hallowed be Thy name," knock, "Thy kingdom come . . ." There was something mechanical in the words and movement; they were soothing. I remembered the prayer, though years had passed since I had said it on my knees. Perhaps kneeling had made me think of it.

"Forgive us our trespasses . . ."

When I had finished I began again.

The rats were quarreling, squeaking, and scurrying in the room. I paid no attention. I forgot everything in the world.

I awoke feeling something soft on my breast, on my cheek. I threw it away with force. A rat thudded to the ground.

Through the barred window and the opaque glass, I saw the blue light of the coming dawn.

XVI

THE BROODER HEN

A SOLDIER took me to the washroom in the morning. I had only begun washing when he knocked at the door. "Hurry up, citizen, give the others a chance."

I had a small basin with me which I filled with water so that I could finish washing in my cell.

It was dark in the cell, the windows were opaque and barred. My paper, pencils, and pens had all been taken away. There was nothing to do. Rats were scratching in the walls. I was not afraid of them now, but I dreaded the night.

At noon the superintendent came.

"Get your things!" And in answer to my questioning look, he added, "you're moving to another cell."

I carried my things in one hand, the basin of water in the other. The superintendent unlocked the last cell in the corridor. There was a group of women at the table. They looked at my basin and laughed.

"Is your name Tolstoy?" an elderly lady with small piercing eyes and a nervous face asked.

"Yes"—but how did she know?

"We are making playing cards out of cigarette boxes. This is your bed," she said, pointing out an empty pallet near the door.

The room was long and of irregular shape, wide at the entrance and narrowing toward the other end. The windows on each side were barred. There was a close-set row of pallets, a table, two chairs. That was all.

"I am a doctor. Petrovskaia is my name," the elderly woman went on. "I was arrested for the Petersburg plot. We were waiting for General Yudenich . . ."

"*Madame parle français, n'est ce pas?*" my neighbor asked me. Her accent, her make-up, and that chic peculiar to the Parisienne showed her nationality.

"Mademoiselle la princesse parle français aussi," she nodded toward a girl of about eighteen with a fine aristocratic face.

"What is the basin for?" a girl with big black eyes asked me. "It looks so funny!"

"It's for washing. Have you got rats here?"

"Not many. The guard brings us a cat once in a while."

I was very sleepy. I made my bed. The pallet consisted of three boards with spaces between them through which the thin mattress of shavings kept slipping. The edges of the boards cut into one's body. I had to put my pillow under my side and use my coat for a pillow. I covered myself with my plaid and fell asleep.

I soon got acquainted with my companions, and got tired of them, as you tire of everybody and everything when you are locked up.

"Enough smoking, Doctor! The cell is full of smoke. There's no air to breathe!" the handsome, phlegmatic typist would grumble, lazily turning on her bed. "And why are you going back and forth like a pendulum?"

"Don't be angry, dear, I can't bear this! My soul aches . . . I have no peace day or night!"

"Well, what's the use worrying? You can't help things. See how quiet I am!"

"Oh! But there's no comparison. You have no family! I have a son and a daughter. I got my husband, who is a professor, mixed up in this business, and he's been arrested, too. Now think! How can I be calm knowing they may all be shot! And it's my fault. I'm responsible."

"You told us they had forgiven your son."

"Oh, well! Do you think anyone can be trusted? I don't. Today they have granted him his life. Tomorrow they may shoot him." And Doctor Petrovskaia tore a piece of cigarette paper, rolled some tobacco and smoked it rapidly.

The typist did not argue.

"You know," said the French woman in her funny broken

Russian, "when you speak to the examining magistrate, you must, well, *enfin, soyez un peu coquette*. A little *rouge* and a little *blanc* on your face, you smile and he begins smiling . . ."

"Did you smile the night they told you to pack up?"

"*O mon Dieu!* No! I did not smile. I wept. I thought they were going to kill me!"

"It was dreadful," Doctor Petrovskaia went on. "When they came and told you to pick up your things, it nearly always meant execution. So once they came and told her to take her things with her. She was frightened to death, and began laughing and crying. Then she threw herself on her knees. 'Doctor,' she said, 'pray for my sinful soul!' I nearly went crazy with her. And in the morning they brought her back."

"Where did they take her?"

"Just to be questioned."

"They try to terrorize the prisoners on purpose," the girl with the large eyes said, "so as to get everything out of them."

"*O mon pauvre Henri! ma pauvre mère! Ils ne sauront jamais ce que j'ai souffert!*"

"She has a fiancé in France," the doctor continued. "She is accused of being a spy. She got intimate with a dishonest man . . ."

"*Mais non, docteur! Pas du tout!* They took me for a spy, and *ce monsieur* saved me. I did not love him, *ce monsieur,* but, oh, *Henri comprendra ça,* I became his . . . *enfin son amante,* out of gratitude. Oh, that was only for a few days . . ."

"It's impossible to understand them," the typist said, shaking up her pillow and making herself comfortable. "I've been listening to them for a whole month and I can't make it out. Why were they arrested and what were the relations between them all?"

"I'll tell you all about it," whispered the doctor in my ear, leaning toward me with the smell of bad tobacco. "Yudenich was approaching Petersburg. There was an Englishman in our organization . . . I lost my head, I was mad . . ."

The doctor spoke quickly, without pausing, as if she had repeated her story many times. I do not know why, but I wanted her to stop and leave me alone. She spoke nervously. Her story was involved and I did not follow her.

"My stepson was shot, perhaps they will spare my son, my daughter is in prison. And I, I alone am to blame. O God!"

She sobbed hysterically. I was ashamed of myself, but I could find no words of consolation. I did not want to listen to her. She made me uneasy. But she spoke, spoke for hours. You could see that everybody in the cell knew her story and was tired of it. They all avoided her, but, once in a while, she would get hold of someone and begin talking again about the Englishman she was in love with and her family. All day long, moistening the tips of her fingers, she would play one game of patience after another, and smoke. She seldom took part in our occupations.

I introduced gymnastics. Every morning, we opened the window as far as the iron bars would allow, stood in a row, and, following Müller's system, made all kinds of movements with our hands, bodies, and feet. I told the French woman that it was good for her health and looks, and she tried hard.

"*Un, deux, trrrois! Un, deux, trrrois!*" she gasped, breathing heavily, the curl papers tossing on her head. Her weak muscles were not used to exercise and every time she had to squat slowly, her feet would not hold her and she would sit down on the floor. It was so funny that we all stopped our exercises and laughed until the guard knocked at the door.

Sometimes the doctor joined us. Her flabby yellow flesh which you could see through the shirt, her false pigtail, all her person was distasteful and pitiful. And when she collapsed on the floor, just as the French woman did, no one laughed.

Once the doctor got very excited. Either she or somebody else noticed that the plaster was loose around the heating pipes which ran from our cell to the neighboring one. I tried to pick it off with a hairpin, and suddenly I heard a rustle from the other side, as if a mouse were scratching.

"Watch the door, will you?" I whispered to my companions.

Doctor Petrovskaia sprang to her feet and took the post of

observation, urging me on. "Try with this," she said, handing
me a knitting needle.

I pushed the needle through, and suddenly it was pulled out
of my hand from the other side of the wall. All my companions, except the doctor, were kneeling beside the heating pipes.
Even the typist was aroused from her usual apathy. The needle
reappeared with a small scrap of paper at the end: "Who are
you? We are . . . (five names)." We knew nearly all of them.
One of them had participated in the meetings at my lodgings.
We answered at once. A correspondence between the two cells
started. I wanted to know how I was to behave at the interro-
gation, for, so far, I had not answered the questions of the police. "Everything is known. There is nothing to be concealed,"
was the answer.

Naïvely thrusting the knitting needle into the hole, I never
suspected that we were following a program that had been
worked out by the administration of the prison; never guessed
that Doctor Petrovskaia was a spy, a "brooder hen,"[1] who was
reporting everything that was going on in our cell. That was
why she was often questioned. It was said that she had bought
the life of her son in this way. Later we were to learn all this—
and that in the other cell, there was also a traitor—Vinogradsky, a childhood friend of two of the members of the Tactical
Center. It was Vinogradsky who, overhearing the conversation
of my friends about the meetings in my rooms, reported it to
the Secret Police and brought about my arrest.

[1] In Soviet prisons this nickname was given to those who gave information or
reported to the examining magistrates the conversations of the prisoners.

XVII

A BRANCH OF MAY

EVERY morning about seven o'clock a large bony Latvian
woman with a very red face opened our door and thrust
a pail of hot water with a dirty rag into our cell with
such force that the water splashed all about. Then she slammed
the door, and we six women in the cell quarreled for the privi-
lege of washing the floor, for that was our only work and pleasure. After about twenty minutes the door opened again, the
silent figure appeared, and the large red hand seized the pail
and pulled it out. In the same way dinner, supper, and hot
water for tea were slung into our cell.

The Latvian never looked at us. Her face was expressionless
and wooden, she spoke shortly as if the mere fact of speaking to
us humiliated her, and she moved stiffly like a crudely-made
puppet.

"She's a machine. Can she possibly laugh or cry or love?" I
thought to myself. And I looked at her with dread. She frightened me more than the prison, the iron bars, the guards, or
even the police magistrates.

The only expression I could detect on her flat face was one of
self-satisfaction, as if she were proud of herself for doing her
duty. She had understood that here in the prison of the Secret
Police what she was expected to do was to lose her human
qualities and become a machine, and she had achieved it perfectly.

Sometimes we tried to talk to her. She did not answer or give
any sign of having heard.

"Has she been trained that way?" I wondered, "or is it her
nature?"

Of course all the employees of the Secret Police were very
well disciplined. But they sometimes acted like human beings,
answered our questions, laughed or quarreled among themselves. And though we saw their roughness and sometimes

their depravity, they had none of the implacable rigidity of this Latvian woman. She was the most terrible being in the prison.

Involuntarily my thoughts followed her. When she entered the room, I could not tear my eyes away from her. I studied her flat coarse face with its white, faded eyebrows and colorless eyes which seemed to look at you without seeing.

"Good morning, comrade!" I was surprised to find myself saying as she thrust the pail of hot water into the cell. With something like astonishment the woman raised her lifeless eyes and then slammed the door without answering.

After that I greeted her every morning, and she pretended not to notice. Once, when she brought our dinner, I offered her some candy, which I had received from friends.

"Not allowed," she said sharply.

Next morning when I greeted her, she bent her head slightly.

"You'll never be able to tame the monster!" my cellmates said. "Why do you bother?"

They laughed and could not see why I should be interested in this being.

But I wanted to find out what the woman really was like, and the more difficult it was, the more I was set upon it. The desire to find something human in her meant so much to me that all my thoughts and will were concentrated on it.

"Good morning! How is the weather today?" I asked her when she entered the room next day.

"Good morning."

I could not believe my ears. This was a victory.

The next Sunday I received a gift of apples. I chose a nice red one and handed it to the woman as she brought in supper.

"Please take it, comrade," I said. "If you don't, you'll offend me."

She hesitated a moment, then snatched the apple from my hand and hid it under her apron. But her face had the same stolid expression. And as she went in and out, brought us things, carried them away, she neither looked at us nor answered our questions.

The twenty-third of April was my name day. Two guards,

smiling, brought me presents from friends. There were so many flowers that we wound the bars with them. It was a real holiday. When the Latvian came, I gave her a bunch of snow-drops. She shrugged her shoulders.

"Please take them," I said, "today is my name day."

She took them without a word. When she brought supper, the flowers were pinned to her breast, but her face was blank.

It happened unexpectedly. One morning, when I awoke and peeked through the crack of the window as I usually did—we could never open the window wide because of the iron bars—I saw a tiny bit of blue sky, and all at once I felt something stir in me. It was spring. All my nature revolted against imprisonment.

I forgot my experiments, and when the Latvian woman came in, I asked her with envy and sadness, as I should have asked anyone who enjoyed freedom, who could look at the sky and the sun:

"Is it fine out today?"

"Yes," she answered. "It is beautiful. It's spring!"

That day, at an unusual time, the door of the cell suddenly opened. The Latvian entered with a wide, bashful smile on her face.

"Citizen Tolstoy!" she said, "this is for you!"

And quickly, as if she were ashamed of herself, she ran away. In my lap was a large blossoming branch of rock cherry.

XVIII

THE VIOLINIST

I WAS miserable. All my fellow prisoners had received something from their friends or their families for Easter, the greatest Russian holiday in the whole year. And I had nothing. Were all my friends in prison? Were they sick? Or had they forgotten all about me?[1]

I was miserable. And yet I knew that it was foolish. I had no sentiment about holidays. I did not even believe in Easter as celebrating the resurrection of Christ. But I longed to be at home and to have painted eggs, a high cake full of raisins (*kulich*), and a *paskha* made out of cottage cheese.

I remembered how when I was a little girl all we children gathered for breakfast on Easter, and mother came out of her room in a white or light gray dress. The table was very large and the cloth so shining and clean that we were afraid to eat on it. On the table were turkey, goose, bacon, ham, and cakes —kulich and paskha. The windows were open; fresh spring air poured into the room from the garden. The church bells rang, from morning till night. There was a whole symphony in the Moscow bells.

And now I was so miserable! There were no more church bells. Moscow was silent. The people were hungry and unhappy, and I was in prison. This dirty cell was like a long grave. Someone's mail, dark cake on a piece of newspaper, three red eggs. And this small kulich, these three painted eggs were worse than nothing. They reminded me of the misery of the people, our own misery . . .

I gave way to my thoughts, and, throwing myself on the bed, turned to the wall and wept.

Everything was silent in the prison. Perhaps my companions were as sad as I; they did not chatter as usual. Not a sound.

---

[1] I learned afterward that all the food that was brought to me that day was kept by the guards.

Suddenly something beautiful and powerful brought me to my feet. All six women sprang up. We rushed to the door, we put our ears to the cracks. Some of us fell to our knees. Silently we listened.

Deep, heavenly sounds broke the stillness. They penetrated the thick stone walls and ceiling, they broke through the roof and soared toward the sun and the sky. They were free and powerful, they alone reigned in the prison.

Somebody was playing a violin. Chopin's "Funeral March." Once, twice. Then the sounds died away and again there was silence in the prison.

We had tears in our eyes. We did not look at each other, we could not speak.

What was it? The music of Chopin played by a great artist. But that had no enormous importance. What was it then? The sound had seemed to go beyond the prison, beyond the iron bars and the walls. Nothing could stop its flight toward infinity. Infinity . . . That was it. That was what it told us about. It told us of the freedom, the power, the beauty of the infinite soul, which knows no bonds, no imprisonment, no end.

Tears of joy were running down my cheeks. I was happy. I knew now that I was free.

Much later, after I was released, I met the typist. We spoke of the time when we were in prison together.

"Do you remember Easter and the violinist?" she asked.

Yes, I remembered.

"He was a great artist," she said. "I was told about him. He was allowed to play only once in prison, and that was when we heard him. The next day he was executed."

XIX

A WORLD APART

THE Latvian told me that we were to be taken to the steam bath on the Tsvetnoy Boulevard. I succeeded in sending word to my friends. Four armed soldiers and the guard with a revolver at his side led us six women. We had to walk in the middle of the street; cabs and automobiles made way for us. Some passers-by looked at us with compassion, others called out "Speculators, thieves!" Others, seeing the painted face of the French woman, and taking us for prostitutes, gave us still uglier names. I was not ashamed. On the contrary, I was rather proud of being a prisoner. Criminals were no longer the conspicuous inmates of prisons.

In spite of the dust and the heat of the city, it was good to breathe in the open air. I had not suspected that the spring was so far advanced. The leaves on the trees had already lost the light yellow green of early spring. They were large and dark.

"Wait a moment! Wait a moment!" a shrill voice shouted. "Political prisoners, aren't you?" and a small fat man jumped from a cab and, crossing the street, ran toward us. "I'm just out of prison myself. I was a political prisoner, too. Don't be disheartened, comrades! Here are some fresh cucumbers for you!"

"Keep off, comrade! We can't allow you to speak to prisoners!"

"And the cucumbers? You'll let me give them to the prisoners?"

"No! Pass on!"

"Oh! That's too bad! But don't lose heart, comrades!" he called. "I've been through it, and I know how you feel!"

"Thank you, thank you for your kind words!" we answered.

Then I saw my friends, sitting as naturally as could be on the grass and sewing. It seemed as if they had just come out of one of the houses to enjoy the air and were calmly doing their mending. As soon as they saw us, they got up and walked along beside us. Perhaps I did not conceal my excitement, or Doctor Petrovskaia had informed the police, but the guard noticed the two ladies at once.

"Keep farther away from the prisoners, citizens!" he shouted, "or I'll arrest you."

One of the ladies was hoping to see her husband, who was in the same prison.

The steam bath was like a military camp, guarded by soldiers. Motorcycles were patrolling in front. As straight as a perch, the commandant was pacing up and down before the building, giving orders to the soldiers and guards.

It was hot and close in the bath, but there was plenty of warm water and we could use any amount of it. We were as red as lobsters when we marched back to the prison. Two ladies were walking on the sidewalk and smiling at us.

I WOKE up in the night. There was a noise behind the wall, as if something heavy had fallen. I heard the guard running along the corridor. For some time everything was quiet; then I heard the steps of several men. They spoke in low voices, breathing heavily as if they were lifting something. They took it out of the cell and carried it along the corridor. I learned later that Gerasimov, Acting Minister of Education in the provisional government, who had lived in our house years before as my brothers' teacher, died that night of heart failure.

"DON'T you smell something burning?" the doctor asked.

We all smelled it. The young princess climbed up the iron bars and looked out into the yard. By leaning to the right, one could see the other side of the yard and part of the prison building.

"I can see smoke," she said. "It looks like fire."

We climbed up in turn and tried to see what was going on. Thick dark smoke was coming from the third floor. The left wing of the building was on fire. Men were shouting in the yard, and we heard the steps of the guards running through the corridor.

"Oh, mercy!" cried the doctor. "Oh! Let's pack!" And she began pulling her bags from under the pallet, tearing off the bedding, and frantically cramming her things in. "They'll come and take us out of the prison. Hurry! We must be ready to go."

The smoke became thicker. It was seeping into our cell.

"I certainly don't want to be burned alive!" cried the French woman, rushing to her cot. Snatching her bedding, her stylish dresses, she began stuffing them into a trunk.

"What's the hurry?" the pretty girl said. "They'll forget all about us." She climbed leisurely down from the window and pulled out her box.

"Oh, no! no! no! You don't really think they'll forget us?"

"Where are all the guards?" cried the French woman, running to the door. *"Sapristi!* Come on, let's try!" And she pushed with all her strength. *"O mon Dieu!* Hallo, hallo! Comrades!"

Nobody answered. We could hear only prisoners running back and forth in their cells and beating on the walls.

"Shut the window quickly!" somebody cried. "The smoke will suffocate us."

We sat on the bare boards of our pallets and waited.

From outside we could hear the shouts of the firemen, automobiles driving into the yard, the sound of running water. The smoke became thicker, the cries of the people in the yard louder and more excited. The noise was dreadful. In our imagination, it grew into a huge and terrible disaster. Our natural instinct to save ourselves had no outlet. We were locked in.

We kept climbing on to the bars to get a glimpse of the firemen running about in their gilt helmets, the soldiers, the engines and hose.

There was less smoke now. As I watched the yard through the crack of the window, a soldier yelled at me. I paid no attention. He shouted again, and, looking in his direction, I saw the barrel of a gun aimed at me. I closed the window and jumped to the floor.

The din quieted, some of the automobiles drove away. We

heard the steps of the guards in the corridor again. Silently we unpacked our things. The excitement was over. Our monotonous everyday life began again.

SUDDENLY the prison shook and the windowpanes rattled. Cannon? Could it be a revolution, a battle starting? The explosions kept on, with the building vibrating until the panes broke and clattered on the floor. We sent a note to our neighbors through the crack between the heating pipes: "What is it?" They did not know. The bursts were regular and frequent. We prayed that it might be a battle, that it might bring us freedom. "Boom! Boom!" and again the building shook. "We shall soon be free. People will come and open the doors!" And we waited.

After some hours the explosions became weaker and less frequent.

"What was it?" we asked the guard in the evening.

"There was a fire in the powder magazines on the Khodynka!" he answered.

XX

WATER!

"WHERE is the hot water?" the doctor asked. The bread and sugar had been brought in as usual but the kettle was missing.

"The water pipes are broken."

"How are we going to chew dry bread?" the pretty typist said, poking at the six dark gray lumps.

"Don't worry, the pipes will soon be repaired," the doctor replied soothingly, "and they will bring us water." She always seemed to know everything.

But no water was brought. There was no soup for dinner; instead, six portions of herring appeared.

"Couldn't you bring water in pails for the prisoners?" I suggested to the guard.

He sniffed disdainfully: "What an idea! Water in pails for all of you! We wouldn't get through in a day!"

"Oh, the devils!" the typist said. "It's the first time they have given us herring, and they pick the very day when there isn't a drop of water! They've done it on purpose! I'll bet they have!"

"*Oh, j'adore les* herrings!" the French woman exclaimed. "And I am going to eat some! *Je m'en fiche!*"

The temptation was great. We were tired of the bad, tasteless food of the prison and we all ate the herrings. But we had to pay for it. In a few hours we were so thirsty that we could hardly stand it; our mouths were parched.

At about four o'clock the guard came: "To the toilet!"

It is impossible to imagine what importance those words had in the Lubianka prison. We were taken to the bathroom only three times a day. The whole procedure was very complicated. The prisoners were not supposed to meet each other in the corridor. There were only a few bathrooms, and the cells were full of prisoners, so the inmates of each cell were taken very seldom and allowed but a short time. In the morning the guard gave us about five or six minutes in the washroom, a very small room with a bathtub, a shower, and a sink. The six of us worked out a system for using every second of our time. We succeeded in bathing and washing some of our clothes as well. One of us immediately got into the bathtub, rubbed herself with soap and stood under the shower. At the same time, while the water was running, we washed our clothes. We could do it in two minutes. Three of us washed in the bathtub; the other three over the sink. The water was icy.

We dried our clothes in the cell, hanging them on a string, and we pressed them with our hands. I never knew you could get such results without an iron. The trick was to start straightening the clothes out when they were just beginning to dry.

At other times we were taken to a toilet where there was not even a place to wash our hands. For this reason I always filled my basin with water so as to be able to wash my face and hands at night.

Usually we were taken to the toilet at about seven or eight, sometimes nine o'clock in the morning. Unfortunately our bowels did not always obey the prison *régime,* and later we would begin knocking at the door:

"Please, let me go to the toilet."

"You've got a close stool . . ."

"You know, comrade, that there is no lid to cover it."

"Do you want to go to solitary? I tell you, there's nothing doing!"

And the guard would walk off to the other end of the corridor. Sometimes the prisoners would writhe for three or four hours, refuse their meals; but the close stool was never used.

When we heard the call: "To the toilet!" on the day the water pipes were out of order, we were very glad, for we hoped to get water somewhere. "Let's take the kettle with us," the doctor said.

The guard opened the door and we saw two armed soldiers standing in the corridor.

"What's the matter? Where are you taking us?"

But the guard walked silently in front of us, one soldier marched beside us and one behind, and nobody answered.

"Examination? Execution? Why are we guarded by soldiers?" Possibilities flashed through my mind.

We were taken downstairs. On the second landing we met an old gray-headed priest in a shabby cassock tightened with a belt around his thin waist. Slowly, dragging his feet, he was climbing upstairs. Two soldiers guarded him. We had to stop on the narrow landing to make way.

The look on the face of the old priest was deeper than suffering. There was forgiveness and understanding in the straight glance of his blue eyes. He wanted to say something, his lips moved, but the words stopped in his throat and suddenly he bowed to us, and we bowed deeply in return. When I lifted my head and looked at him, his eyes were beaming. Slowly, under the guard of armed soldiers, he moved on.

We were led into the dirty yard of the prison. As I waited my turn near the door of the toilet, I looked at the sky. I had never known that one could feel such joy in seeing it!

"Too bad!" one of the young soldiers sighed. "I'm sorry for him!"

"For whom?"

"He's old, that priest! And what can he have done to them?"

Upon our return to the cell I was summoned for questioning. In a soft leather armchair, a fat smug official, Agranov, was sitting. This was the second time he had examined me. He had been very polite the first time, offered me cigarettes, and asked me how I liked it in prison. Then, taking a pile of papers and pointing to them, he had said:

"I want to inform you, Citizen Tolstoy, that your friends are wiser than you are. Long ago they told me all about your rôle in the plot. Here is their testimony," and he named one of my friends. "He has not spared you in his statements!"

"Don't you think that your methods of questioning are rather old-fashioned?" I interrupted. "This is just the way the

Secret Police questioned the revolutionaries in the time of the Tsar."

"As you like!" the magistrate retorted. "I only wanted to help you out and make things easier for you and your friends!"

"Are you a long-standing member of the party?"

"I don't think that has anything to do with our present conversation."

"Yes, it has. Did the old government persecute you?"

"Yes, but I don't understand . . ."

"Did you betray your friends and relatives to help yourself out?"

He rang the bell. "Take the citizen to her cell. We shall see what you'll say when you have spent several months more with us!"

This time again I did not intend to answer him. I was gloomy and silent.

"What's the matter with you?" he asked. "You seem to have lost some of your energy."

"Do you know that the prisoners haven't had a drop of water all day long and were given herring for dinner?"

"Is that so?"

But I was certain that he knew all about it.

"It's a form of torture! How can you . . ."

"A cup of tea!" Agranov called out. "Will you have a cigarette?" He laid a cigarette case politely before me.

"I will not answer! I don't want your tea! Can't you give an order for water to be sent to the cells?"

The cup of tea standing on the table only excited my thirst and powerless anger.

"You won't answer? We'll wait a little longer and see if you're easier to handle."

We got hot water for supper.

AFTER two months in prison I was set free quite unexpectedly. I packed up my things and said goodbye. As I was about to leave the cell I suddenly had an idea, and wrote in big black letters on the white wall opposite the door the thought that came to me when I was listening to the "Funeral March": "The Holy Spirit in every one of us is free. No bars, no guards, no prison walls can deprive us of our Freedom!"

XXI

THE PROSECUTOR

SEVERAL of those who were less deeply involved in the plot were let out of prison at the same time. The leaders were held, and a number of others—about twenty in all —most of them professors or literary men.

My feeling on leaving prison was like the sensation one has on landing after a long sea voyage. I was unsteady, undecided; and I could not settle down to my everyday work at the museum and Yasnaia Poliana. I could think of nothing but the approaching trial. Would my friends, the five men who were chiefly implicated, be executed or not?

I was afraid to meet the relatives and wives of those five. There was always one question in their eyes: "Do you think there is hope?"

On a table in the annex of the Supreme Court of Justice, far away from the center of Moscow, files of papers were lying. Here the accused could get acquainted with the case and read the detailed testimony of Professor Kotliarevsky and others. I had neither the time nor the desire to read it all; my connection with the case was only accidental. But I learned here of the treachery of the miserable hysterical woman, Petrovskaia. And I discovered that my arrest had resulted from the conversation of one of my friends with Vinogradsky.

Across the street, in the yard of a fine apartment, a short heavily built man could be seen striding with a whip in his hand, giving orders to servants in the loud voice of one who is conscious of his power. He was surrounded by a number of hunting dogs. Krylenko, the prosecutor, was a sportsman and he was going hunting.

XXII

THE TRIAL

THE trial took place in the Polytechnic Museum where I used to attend lectures and concerts. There were many familiar faces in the crowd. The accused were seated on the front benches, the judges at a big table, covered with a blood red cloth, and the private and government lawyers on the left. Many of the private lawyers had been men of reputation, some of them had once been revolutionists; now they were considered enemies of the people and they made a pitiful impression—especially one of them, who lifted his hands to his face as if begging to be understood. The judges rudely interrupted his eloquence, the government lawyers smiled.

The government lawyers, ignorant, ungifted people who were acquainted with the judges and familiar with the new methods of jurisprudence, now played the main rôle. The brilliant pleaders of the old days, who could stir their listeners to pity or indignation and soften the hearts of the judges, were powerless. And skill, knowledge, and logic were dispensed with.

At a small separate table to the right sat the prosecutor, Krylenko, with his smooth head and massive jaw, reminding one of a savage dog that needed to be kept muzzled. He looked bloodthirsty, hungry for victims. His voice was like metal; he chopped his words and they resounded splendidly, carrying into every corner of the great hall.

There was no use in pleading not guilty. A few of the accused, such as Vinogradsky and Professor Kotliarevsky, had turned state's evidence and confessed everything. Krylenko did not conceal his contempt for the fawning, flattering way they answered the judges. Their activities would very likely earn them pardons and even promotion. Khiriakov, who composed a poem about the trial, described them creeping on all fours and singing to the judges: "You are ours, we are yours, and we love you so much . . ."

My attention was so concentrated on the group who were on trial for their lives that I almost forgot that I was one of the accused. I was still free. I had come from home, I walked freely about the hall, and talked with friends. It came as a surprise to me when an agent of the police ordered me to sit on the front bench under guard with the other accused. That evening when the court adjourned all of us were taken to the Lubianka prison.

We had with us not so much as a comb. But Nikolai Mikhailovich Kishkin, a well-known doctor, had a knapsack on his back. They put us all in a big dirty cell with a lot of bare wooden cots. Everybody was excitedly discussing the trial. Nikolai Mikhailovich opened his bag and took out tea, sugar, and black rusks.

"What does this mean?" I asked. "How did you know we would be arrested today?"

"Well, there's nothing surprising in that, Alexandra Lvovna. How many times have you been arrested?"

"Three."

"That is not much. I have had much more experience. I have lost count of the times I've been in prison. I went to prison during the old *régime,* and I keep it up now. I've been taking this bag to the court for several days."

The guard brought hot water, bread, and sugar. We all had tea. In a far corner sat the bent figure of Vinogradsky. No one offered him tea.

"It's awkward, though," one of the professors said. "We ought to ask him . . ."

No one answered. The professor got up and went over to Vinogradsky.

I stretched out on my cot and put my hand under my head for a pillow, but no sooner did I close my eyes than I felt a sharp bite. The boards were full of bugs. Right and left professors were tossing about and groaning.

"Oh, the devil take them! It's no use trying to sleep," someone sighed, turning from one side to the other.

But Kishkin made his bed comfortably, spreading his pillow
and blanket on the cot, and fell asleep as if he were at home.
And the mutterings of the professors did not prevent me from
sleeping, too.

We awoke in the morning tired and pale, with lined faces.
My white dress looked like a dirty rag. We washed our hands
and faces without soap, dried them with our pocket handkerchiefs, combed our hair with our fingers, and, surrounded by
guards, walked to the Polytechnic Museum.

Pardon or death for those five men? Probably the verdict
had already been dictated by the government; the questions of
the lawyers seemed stereotyped. In contrast every word of the
accused rang out with emphasis.

"I never worked for any government. But I have worked all
my life for the entire people," Kishkin concluded. His brilliant
defense was received with applause. The audience seemed to
have forgotten where they were, and the judge roughly reminded them:

"Anyone who causes a disturbance will be expelled from the
hall."

The excitement became most intense when the five were to
be questioned: five good-looking young men, all of them talented, honest, energetic, and each in his own way learned.

Suddenly there was a stir in the hall. Everyone began moving about and conversing in whispers, even the judges. A number of people came in and scattered among the audience, and
the peaked helmets of the Secret Police appeared in the corri-
dors and doorways. A man with a pointed black beard and a
shock of hair, protruding ears, and glasses on his nose, entered
the hall, and began to speak calmly and self-confidently. It was
Leo Trotsky, Commissar of War. He spoke about one of the
five, a young scientist. People like this young man were necessary to the Republic, he said. His work was known. It was
brilliant. When Trotsky had finished and left the hall, there

was confusion for a few minutes. The guards at the doors vanished, together with the civilians who had come in just before the speech.

It now became evident that the chances of saving the five from death were better. I could never understand why the man who at this time possessed such unlimited power, by whose orders thousands were executed in Crimea, wanted to save the young scientist.

The trial went on.

"Citizen Tolstoy," Krylenko asked me, "what was your rôle in the Tactical Center?"

"My rôle," I answered in a loud voice, "my rôle consisted in heating the samovar for the members of the Tactical Center."

"And serving tea?"

"Yes, and serving tea."

"That was the only part you had in the business?"

"Yes."

The audience laughed and the prosecutor was ruffled. This dialogue evoked the following verses from Khiriakov:

> O citizens! Move with care
> In a country where a bold maiden
> Is put into a narrow cell
> For heating a samovar!
>
> Let a hundred tortures threaten me!
> I do not fear disaster.
> In defiance of Soviet power
> I'll always heat my samovar!

The five were only nominally sentenced to death; in actual fact they got ten years' imprisonment. All the others were sentenced to prisons and camps for different periods. Vinogradsky and several others were released. I was given three years in a prison camp. It did not matter to me. I was happy not to be with those who were set free.

XXIII

"YOU CAN BE HAPPY ANYWHERE"

SOLDIERS led us out of the prison into the court—the pretty girl with thick fair hair and dark blue eyes and me. It was sultry and hot; we had to wait in the yard. Other prisoners who had been condemned to various prisons and camps as a result of the trial were being led out by the guards. We exchanged greetings, and said goodbye. Then two armed soldiers led us away.

A heavy bag weighed on my shoulders. It was hard to walk in the middle of the cobblestone streets, and after several miles our feet were blistered. The heat became more and more unbearable, and we had to go to the other end of the city.

"Comrades," said the pretty girl to the soldiers, "please let us walk on the sidewalk, our feet are so sore."

"Not allowed."

The clouds thickened, the sky grew dark. We went very slowly, though the "comrades" hastened us. The air became heavier and heavier. A drop of rain fell on my face and then another. At first the drops were large and infrequent. Then the sky was torn by a sharp flash of lightning, thunder reverberated between the stone walls, and the rain began to pour. It cleared and purified the air, and washed the dust off the dirty streets and houses. Streams flowed in the gutters. People hurried past us.

"Stop a moment," one of the soldiers said. "We'll wait till it's over." And he made for a sheltered archway.

I got out my cigarette case, and held it out to the men.

"Have a smoke?"

They smiled and I felt as if for a moment they had become more human.

I took off my shoes and stockings, washed my swollen feet under the drain pipe, and felt much better.

The rain was over. The sun, breaking through a blue-black cloud, shone on the wet pavements, the roofs of the houses, the leaves of the few trees.

"Citizens!" our guard said, "you can go on the sidewalk. Your feet look as if they were scalded."

We were much more comfortable walking barefoot on the smooth asphalt.

"Did you get a long sentence?" one of the soldiers asked.

"Three years."

"Bad luck! Your youth will be wasted."

I glanced at the girl. She was quite young, about twenty-five; I was thirty-eight. Three years in prison . . . That was certainly a long time . . .

At last we reached the ancient, high-walled Novospasky Monastery, now a prison camp. Two soldiers guarded the entrance.

"Two more!" cried our guards. "Here they are!"

One of the soldiers got up lazily from a bench. A bunch of keys clanked, the big lock grated as the key turned. We were let in and the old gate closed after us slowly and silently.

As we walked, I looked around. On the left was a cemetery with battered monuments and blistered iron crosses. On the other side were the low white monastery buildings and old shade trees. The air was full of the bitter-sweet fragrance of poplar leaves.

I felt as if I knew this place. Its quiet and solemnity took hold of me as they always had when my mother had taken me to ancient monasteries in my childhood.

"You slut!"

Two women came running around the corner of a building. Their faces were flushed with anger, their hair was disheveled. The older woman had seized her companion by the hair, while the younger one cursed and tried to bite her.

A guard ran past us, pushing us aside.

"Stop fighting, you bitches!" he cried, tearing the women apart.

Scolding and cursing and smoothing their hair, the women disappeared.

We entered the office. Perhaps because of the fatigue of the journey, perhaps because of the scene I had just witnessed, my knees trembled.

"And I shall have to stay here for three years with such women," I thought to myself.

A handsome Jewish girl with short curly hair was writing at a table. A middle-aged woman, wearing a plain cotton blouse, rough homemade skirt, and felt slippers on her bare feet, got up from another table and beckoned to us, smiling.

"Please come here. I must register you. Your family name? Age? Your family name is Tolstoy? What is your first name? Father's name?"

"Alexandra—Lvovna," I answered.

For a second she raised her eyes; then she went on with her questions.

Lighting a cigarette and swinging her hips, the handsome Jewess left the room.

Immediately the face of the other woman changed. She seized my hand and shook it warmly.

"Are you the daughter of Lev Nikolayevich? Oh!"

I was hardly listening. The violent scene outside had thoroughly upset me, and I was in no mood to answer banal questions about my father.

"Are these all criminals?" I asked. "How beastly it all is!"

"Dear Alexandra Lvovna," she said, "don't be distressed, please don't. We can live anywhere—it all depends on ourselves. And this place is not so dreadful as it seems at first. Believe me, you can be happy anywhere. Come, I'll show you to your cell. Let me help you carry your things."

She had a soft, deep voice.

"Will you tell me your name?" I asked.

It was familiar to me.

"Are you related to ——, the governor?"

"Yes."

"That is why you are in prison?"

"Yes," and she smiled wistfully.

A little woman with bobbed hair, carrying an armful of linen, met us.

"Anna Fedorovna," said the governor's daughter, "have we got a spare cot in our room? This is the daughter of Tolstoy. Let's take her in our cell."

The little woman smiled and nodded.

"Come."

Again to our left the ancient graves and to our right the old white buildings of the monastery.

"Here we are. Upstairs, on the second floor. Keep to your right."

I pushed the door open and entered a little room with a low ceiling, unpainted floor, small windows and a stove of ancient blue-rimmed tiles—the cell of a monk in bygone days. And again I felt the peace of the monastery.

A tall dark old woman in a neat black cotton dress with white dots and a white shawl tied under her chin got up from her bed and bowed.

"Aunt Liza," said Anna Fedorovna, "did you ever hear of Lev Tolstoy?"

"Yes, certainly," she said, "I always had great respect for him."

"Well, this is his daughter."

"A strange place to meet her," sighed the old woman. "But God knows what He is doing!" And again she bowed and sat down.

She had a noble face and a clear happy smile. "More the face of a saint than of a criminal," I thought. "Why can she be in prison?"

"Put your things here," said Anna Fedorovna, who I learned had been chosen by the prisoners as a sort of leader, and she showed me an empty cot beside Aunt Liza's.

Suddenly the door opened, and a tall very prim lady came in with light quick steps. Her hair was smooth and gray, and she wore an old-fashioned tight-waisted dress. One could see that she had been very beautiful in her youth.

"Let me introduce myself," she said. "I am ——"

"Are you Baroness ——?" I asked.

"*Chut! Plus de baronnes maintenant! C'est à cause de cela que je souffre,*" she whispered. "But why are you in prison? Your father was known to the world as a radical—an a-nar-chist." She pronounced it with some difficulty and distaste.

"I am accused of counterrevolution," I said.

"*Affreux!*"

Anna Fedorovna went to get hot water for tea.

I watched my cellmates with the greatest interest. Aunt Liza drank her tea from the saucer, as if she were performing a very important rite, slowly and in a business-like way, as the Russian peasants do. The baroness brought a pretty cup from her room and drank hers daintily, crooking her little finger. The governor's daughter took boiled water and a crust of bread.

"Why don't you drink tea?" I asked.

"You don't know her," Anna Fedorovna said. "She is begin-ning to swell from hunger, and she hasn't a drop of blood in her, yet she gives all her food away—her butter, sugar, oil—everything she gets from the Red Cross."[1]

"Dear Anna Fedorovna, please don't talk about me," said the governor's daughter. The blood rushed to her pale face and she frowned. "Please don't pay any attention to me."

When I went to bed the thought which had haunted me all these last days came to me again, "I am sentenced to prison for three years!" To my surprise it did not make me wretched as it had before. I began thinking about my cellmates—Aunt Liza with her grave, saintly face, the beautiful yellow hair and gen-tle eyes of the governor's daughter. I heard her soothing voice: "You can be happy anywhere."

"She is right," I thought to myself. There was no fear or loneliness in my heart as I closed my eyes.

[1] The Political Red Cross, a social institution, organized by the Russian intelli-gentsia under the control of the Soviet Government to help political prisoners.

XXIV

THE MONK

I AWOKE in the middle of the night. From close by came sounds of iron striking on stone. Someone awoke in the next room.

"Oh! the girls are at their work again!"

"What did you say? What is it?" I asked. But nobody answered.

The sounds continued—the blunt strokes of a crowbar, spades clanking against stone. It seemed to me that something unpleasant was going on. And this something which I sensed yet did not comprehend troubled me.

In the morning I questioned Anna Fedorovna.

"Some of the girls," she answered, "the thieves and prostitutes—dig the coffins out of the graves, looking for treasure. The guards shouldn't allow it, but I suppose they get their share. Perhaps I ought to tell the commandant. But it's no use. They're all alike, the convicts, the guards, and the commandant. And if I speak about it, all the criminals will have it in for me."

"Do they find anything?" I asked.

"Certainly—gold rings, bracelets, and crosses, and sometimes precious stones and diamonds. The cemetery is very old, you know, and rich people were buried in it."

I went out to see. The yard was full of graves. Not far from the monastery was the grave of Princess Tarakanova,[1] and farther on was an unornamented vault where the first Romanovs were buried. Two women were playing cards on a black marble slab. Near by was an open grave. Pieces of wood, human bones, and freshly dug earth were scattered about.

"What is all this?" I asked.

[1] Princess Tarakanova was the morganatic daughter of the Empress Elizabeth. She was made a nun by order of Catherine the Great.

"The girls were working here last night," one of the women answered.

"Don't you think it is a sin?" I asked, just to say something.

"A sin? Why, no. They need nothing now," and she pointed to the bones. "The girls will enjoy the jewels. But I don't think they found anything last night."

I lay awake the next night, listening to the blows of the crow-bar and the clank of the spades. The sounds went on for several nights. One night they ceased, and something else began—in-human yells like the screams of the insane. We rushed to the room they came from. Several hysterical women were throw-ing themselves on the floor, shrieking and drowning out the angry cries of the guards.

Turning up skulls and pulling rings and bracelets from the dry hands of the dead had become too much for the nerves of these women, poisoned as they were by cocaine and alcohol. Hallucinations tormented them and the dead followed them. Every evening at twilight they saw a shadow which took the form of a man, a monk in a gray robe, float slowly into the room through the iron bars. They shrank away from the ter-rible vision and covered their faces with their hands. And then this general hysteria began.

The madness of this cell soon infected the others. The mys-terious monk was seen in nearly all the cells. Not only the criminals but the political prisoners declared that they had seen him.

One evening we all went to the prison theater. Only the baroness and another woman, whom we did not like very much and who had recently come to our cell, stayed away. This lady was nervous, capricious, always fussing about some-thing, and sometimes we grew very tired of her. When we got back to the cell she was highly excited.

"Do you know what has happened!" she exclaimed as soon as we came in. "I went to Anna Fedorovna's room to get a book, and who do you suppose was sitting on her bed?"

"The monk."

"Yes, but how did you know? It was the monk. I thought he

was real. I asked him if he had come to see Anna Fedorovna and if I might do something for him. And he raised his eyes, looked at me, and smiled. I felt uncomfortable and left the room, but I couldn't keep quiet. I went in again. He was still sitting in the same position. Suddenly I realized he was a ghost. I shut the door and went and called the baroness. When we opened the door, he was gone."

A few days passed. One night when we were getting ready for bed a door slammed.

The nervous lady jumped to her feet. "Who's there?"

"I don't know," Anna Fedorovna replied. "I think everybody's in."

Yes, we were all there.

I got up and looked out. There was no one on the stairs. Even down in the yard no one was to be seen.

"It was the monk," whispered the nervous lady, "I am sure it was the monk."

"It's nerves, nerves, my dear lady," retorted Anna Fedorovna, as she bent to unlace her shoes.

Aunt Liza sighed deeply and made the sign of the cross.

XXV

GEORGE

WHO is that?" I asked Anna Fedorovna, as a strange masculine-looking person, wearing a soldier's cloak and high boots, passed us. "Is it a man or a woman?"

"Oh, that's George. She's often taken for a man. She is a very interesting person. Wait, I'll call her! Hallo, George!"

"At your orders, Anna Fedorovna."

"Won't you come and see us some time?"

"Thanks, I'll come this evening!"

"A very interesting person," repeated Anna Fedorovna. "She has been convicted sixteen times for theft, but as you can see it hasn't dampened her spirits. She is very clever—she's musical, sings, and has a big voice. We'll ask her to sing tonight. Oh, she has many talents. She has been a singer in beer gardens, an acrobat in the circus, and she is as strong as a bull!"

"Anna Fedorovna!" I interrupted, laughing, "you speak of this monster as if you liked her."

"Yes? Well, perhaps I do. She's an exceptional person and she has her own original understanding of honesty."

"I should think it was original—a woman convicted of theft sixteen times."

"All right, but she's one of the few people I trust. She looks on theft as a trade, but in her everyday life she's honest, not like all these hooligans. I have known her since Butyrki.[1] We were there at the same time. She made a terrible row. There was a young girl imprisoned for political reasons, I believe. She got sick. George nursed her and was very fond of her, followed her about like a devoted dog, did everything she could for her. Well, somebody insulted the girl, and she began to cry. George got furious. She lost her temper and pitched into the fellow.

---

[1] Butyrki is the largest Moscow prison.

Nobody could manage her. Finally the guards seized her and put her in solitary. There were straw mattresses in her cell. She piled them up and set fire to them, and then shouted with all her might. When they got her out, she was nearly suffocated.

"For a while she was a nurse in the prison hospital, and a good one, too. The patients liked her, but she quarreled with her chief and was taken away. You have no idea how skilful she is! She can unlock a door with two teaspoons."

"How long has she been here?"

"About a year. But she has an exceptional position. The commandant sends her out to work."

"What kind of work?"

"Jobs in her line—stealing. You see the commandant and she have an agreement. Everything George gets must be divided between them. Sometimes he gives her special orders. The other day he wanted a pine marten fur. She brought a fur, but it wasn't sable, it was skunk. She couldn't find a sable, she said.

"George isn't selfish. She always shares things. Once when the commandant sent her out, she got hold of a pair of horses somewhere in the suburbs. She was leading them to the camp early in the morning when a policeman stopped her. 'Where did you get these horses?' he asked. 'From the camp. I had them shod,' she answered. 'That's likely,' said the policeman. 'Nobody shoes horses at this hour. Come along!' And he brought her to the camp. The commandant caught on to the situation at once. 'Are these horses yours?' the policeman asked. 'Yes,' answered the commandant. The policeman had to go away. George got one horse as her share and gave it to the prisoners. They ate it, and the other . . ."

"But this is nonsense!" I exclaimed. "It's incredible."

"Nonsense? All the camp knows about it, and if you don't believe me, there is the commandant's horse!" And Anna Fedorovna pointed to a thin dapple-gray animal that was browsing assiduously among the graves.

In the evening George came to visit us.

"Well, here I am," she announced.

We gathered around the table and drank tea, talking a little guardedly at first, with our guest. Feeling herself in polite company, George behaved with a somewhat elaborate propriety.

Dunia, a quiet, pious girl who had never been anywhere outside her native village, watched her with amazement and fear. Dunia was in the same cell with the governor's daughter and looked to her for protection from the city girls who persecuted her and called her a "servant of the nobles." She was shocked at our inviting this "shameless lost creature" to our cell. The baroness, too, was shocked and uncomfortable in George's society, but she was lonely in her tiny dark room. She came to see George as she would have gone to the theater. The governor's daughter came and went. She was always busy. George evoked in her neither horror nor disgust, only deep compassion.

Aunt Liza was more disturbed than any of us. She could not bear the presence of this woman who had sunk so far below anything she could understand. George's every word and movement disgusted her. The old woman poured herself a mug of tea and went into the next room.

George soon got over any embarrassment and began exhibiting her talents. Suddenly she stood up and sang an aria from an opera in a loud hoarse voice. She passed on to a light chansonette, and, lifting her feet very high, began dancing the cancan.

"Abominable!" muttered the baroness.

"God save us sinful creatures!" groaned Aunt Liza from the other room.

Now George underwent another transformation. Her neck swelled, her face became suffused with blood, and straining every muscle, she pretended to lift a two-hundred-pound weight from the floor. The muscles of her arms swelled to enormous balls, and she groaned. At last she threw out her hand, as if she had the weight in it, and balancing by planting her feet wide apart, she marched through the room.

"Splendid! Bravo, bravo!" we exclaimed.

"George, tell us about some of your adventures," said Anna Fedorovna.

"All right," she said, "but I'm so thirsty."

"Have some tea."

"Tea! That's good for chickens! Well, there is nothing for it. Shall I tell you about the samovar?"

Crossing her legs and wiping her large face and greasy nose, she began:

"This was in the old days. There were two crowds of us working and we were having—you know—a competition. Well, once we got together in a tavern, and our crowd began boasting about what we'd taken. 'Hold on,' one of the others said, 'we'll show you something.' And they got out a great silver samovar.

" 'Sure, it's a good samovar,' I said, 'but where's the lid?'

" 'There isn't any.'

" 'Rot!' I said. 'Where is it?'

" 'Well, there was an alarm in the general's house where we took it, and the lid got left behind.'

" 'Fu-u-u,' I whistled disdainfully. 'The pot's all right, but what's it worth without the lid? Nothing!'

" 'Well, try and get the lid, if you're so clever.'

" 'All right, I'll get it.'

" 'We bet you don't.'

" 'I will!' I said, already shaping up a plan.

"And so we agreed that if I got the lid, I'd get the samovar, too, and the other party would stand the drinks, and if I lost, they could have anything of mine they wanted, and I'd pay for the party.

"When we left the inn, my crowd all told me: 'You were a fool to boast like that. Everyone in the house will be on the watch.'

" 'Just hold your tongues, and take orders,' I said. 'Come on to the "fence"!' He gets us everything we need. 'Give us two costumes,' I said, 'one for a policeman and the other for a police inspector!'

"Next morning I put on the inspector's uniform and a friend the policeman's. In pants you'd never guess I was a woman.

We went to the front door of the general's house and rang the
bell . . ."

"O George, this can't be the truth," Anna Fedorovna interrupted.

"On my honor, Anna Fedorovna. I'll make the sign of the
cross if you wish."

"O God," came Aunt Liza's voice from the next room, "for
mercy's sake don't make the sign of the cross! You have enough
sins on your conscience."

"All right, Aunt Liza, don't groan. Only I'm telling you the
truth. Well, we went in. A servant in a white apron opened the
door.

" 'How shall I announce you?' she asked.

" 'Tell His Excellency that the police inspector wants to see
him on a very important matter,' I answered.

"In a few minutes the general came out—a stout man with a
big bass voice—and he rumbled, 'What's the matter? What do
you want?' We stood in front of him saluting.

" 'Allow me to report to Your Excellency,' I said, 'on a matter which concerns Your Excellency.'

" 'What matter?'

" 'About your samovar which was stolen.'

" 'Well, do you know something about it?'

" 'It is not quite certain yet, Your Excellency. The samovar
in question has no lid.'

" 'Yes, yes,' the general exclaimed joyfully. 'It must be mine;
the thieves didn't take the lid.'

" 'Your Excellency,' I said, 'may we have the lid, please?
We will try it, and if it fits, we'll know that the samovar belongs to Your Excellency and we will bring it to you within
an hour.'

"The general was delighted. He called the maid and told
her to bring the lid of the silver samovar. We took it and
cleared out.

"When I got back to the crowd it was my turn to laugh.
'Well, how would you like a good party, and something

stronger than water to go with it?' I asked. 'And now that we've earned the samovar, we'll sell it for a good price with the cap on its head!' "

"Mais c'est du talent!" exclaimed the baroness. Her sympathies were obviously not on the side of the general.

George drank a mug of tea at a draught, and lit a cigarette.

"This one was after the Revolution," she said, "when the Soviet started nationalizing private property. There was a panic among the Moscow merchants. Goods were sold for nothing.

"I was going around Moscow then. I had no money and no job, and I didn't want to sell my clothes—they were good at that time, and I had some jewels on me, too. I looked like a lady all right!

"I was wandering about the streets when I saw a sign, 'Wood sold cheap.' I went into the yard. The owner came up.

" 'How do you do!' she said. 'What can I do for you?'

" 'I need some wood,' I said.

" 'How much do you want?'

" 'About ten cords. But your price is very high.'

"The woman was offended: 'How can you say that, madam?' she said. 'The wood's shamefully cheap. It's only bad times that make me sell at such a low price! You see, I'm all alone, my husband never came back from the war. I've made my living by this woodyard, and now they say that all the yards are to be nationalized, so I'm selling out.'

"Well, we made a bargain. I wrote down her telephone number and promised to call her later and say where I wanted her to deliver the wood.

" 'Not a bad beginning,' I thought to myself. And I hoped it would work out. I was hungry, so I went to the Paris Tavern. I made myself comfortable and with the air of a great lady I ordered steak—oh, I love a rare steak—and a cup of coffee. They brought me the meal. I didn't hurry. I took my time eating and began a conversation with the innkeeper. 'Things aren't going well,' I said, 'all the goods are being taken away from honest folks.'

" 'Are you a merchant?' the host asked. 'Yes, I sell wood.'

The man seemed to be interested. It turned out that he needed wood and he asked me the price. I quoted a price that was lower than the one I had agreed on with the woman. I saw his eyes sparkle. He knew damned well that the price was low, and he thought he had a good bargain.

" 'Is the wood dry?' he asked.

" 'Certainly, it was cut last year.' After questioning me a long time, he said he wanted to buy eight cords. I went calmly to the telephone—oh, you know you have to be a good actor, too —'Hello, hello!' I said. 'Hello,' said the owner of the woodyard, 'who is it speaking?'

" 'I'm speaking from the Paris Tavern.'

" 'Who is speaking?'

" 'The owner!'

"The host of the inn thought I was the owner of the wood-yard and the woman at the woodyard took me for the hostess of the inn.

" 'Bring me eight cords of birch wood as soon as possible!' I ordered. And I gave the address.

"The woman recognized my voice and said:

" 'But, madam, I can only bring you four today and four to-morrow. I have no more carts.'

" 'All right,' I said, 'but hurry.'

"I asked for some boiled sturgeon with horseradish and went on eating. I waited more than two hours. At last the wood was brought. The host went into the yard to show the drivers where to put it.

"To tell you the truth I was pretty nervous. But in a few minutes he came back. He looked pleased and rubbed his hands. 'Your wood is good,' he said, 'very good.'

" 'Well, and how about the payment? It's time for me to go.' 'All right,' he said, 'I can pay you.' 'Well,' I said, 'now that I have done you a favor by selling you such splendid wood, I'll ask a favor of you. I would never have sold it at such a price, if I didn't have a bill to pay tomorrow morning. So I wish you'd pay me for all the eight cords right away. The rest will be delivered tomorrow.' The host agreed.

"I counted the money, gave him a receipt, paid him for my dinner, and went out into the yard.

"'Hello, men!' I cried to the drivers. 'Pile that wood properly!'

"'All right!' they answered. 'Give us a tip, and we'll do our best.'

"They thought I was the hostess of the tavern.

"I sauntered out into the street and then—I took to my heels. Do you believe me? Next day I sent a boy to see how they got out of the muddle. But the boy was a fool. He didn't learn anything and he nearly got caught. And that's all the story."

For a few minutes there was silence in the room. Nobody laughed.

"George," I said, "have you ever tried to live honestly?"

Her face became sullen—nearly angry.

"Yes. I can't live an honest life. I always want to steal. There was a time when I didn't steal for several months. I felt terrible! Then I met friends, and I couldn't help it, I began again."

"Aren't you sorry sometimes?" asked the governor's daughter.

"Yes, sometimes. Only you mustn't think that I take anything from the poor. I only rob the rich. And as for killing— God preserve me from that!"

"How did you begin to steal?"

"I don't remember. That was a long time ago. Did you ever hear of Sashka Seminarist?"[2] A note of pride came into her voice. "Well, he was my teacher. I began working with him. I am from Petersburg. My parents were very poor. At first they decided to give me a good education and sent me to the high school, but they couldn't afford to keep me there. They took me out of the fifth class and married me to a rich old man. He was seventy, and yet he was so vile . . . I can't tell you about him. I couldn't bear him. I stole a hundred rubles from him and ran off. Where could I go? I was only seventeen. I

---

[2] A well-known robber in Petersburg, who eluded capture for many years.

went to an inn. I was afraid and all alone. There I met
Sashka . . .

"But why do you make me think of it! Give me another
cigarette." She lit it and inhaled deeply. "I'm in my forties now.
There's no use changing. I'll be shot one day under a fence like
a dog, or I'll die in prison . . . Doesn't it come out even anyway?"

And again her face became dark and angry.

Gently, as if to soothe her, the governor's daughter put her
hand on the woman's shoulder.

SEVERAL days later George disappeared from camp. We thought
the commandant had sent her out to work.

"What's the matter with George?" we asked each other.
"She never stayed away so long before. Perhaps she's been
caught."

She returned on the fourth day empty handed and very cross,
she refused to speak to anyone or answer questions.

Finally she came to our cell.

"I am hungry," she said sulkily, "and I have no tobacco.
Give me some *makhorka*.[3] I'm a beggar. The prison food is
enough to kill you. I've got to ask the commandant to let me
go to work again."

"Didn't you get anything the last time?"

"No! I was caught by the police."

"You don't mean it!"

"Don't I mean it!" she retorted. "Thank God, I'm back. I
thought I was lost, and it was all the fault of some damned
music . . ."

"What music?"

"A clock with music. Wait a minute," and she bit greedily
into a large slice of black bread with bacon. "I'll tell you all
about it."

When the slice of bread and bacon had disappeared, and she
had lit a cigarette, her good humor returned.

[3] A cheap tobacco.

"The commandant told me to bring him a clock," she began. "Well, the other day I didn't get him the fur he wanted, so I thought I'd please him with the clock. Long ago I noticed a flat where some rich Jews—Communists—lived. They had good clothes, silver, lots of things, and good things, too. In the morning, the man and his wife usually went to the office, and the servant went to market. The flat was empty an hour or two. Well, that was the time I called on them. Oh, I took everything I liked—clothes and linen and a few silver things—as much as I could carry. I tied them up in a blanket, and put the clock on the top of the bundle so as not to hurt it. I loaded the bundle on my back and went out. As I went through the archway, I met a servant. She looked at me suspiciously.

" 'Where are you coming from?' she asked.

" 'I am a laundress,' I said, 'I've taken the linen from Number Eight,' and I hurried along.

"Suddenly the damned clock began playing 'In the garden, in the orchard.'

" 'Stop, stop!' cried the servant, running after me. 'That's our clock!'

"I ran and she chased me. A janitor ran out; then another. They began whistling, and finally a policeman caught me. Well, they took away my things and brought me to the police station. They kept me three days. By good luck one of the policemen knew me. I shook all the money I had out of my stocking and gave to them. They let me go. But I didn't get a thing, and I lost the money I had. I'm hungry. I have to beg for tobacco and bread—worse than a beggar. And now the commandant won't let me work. 'What if you are caught again?' he says, 'I'll be in a fine mess.' But I think I'll go and ask him again, anyway."

XXVI

POOR PLEASURES

O RLOVA! Manka! Visitors!" someone shouted under the windows.

Manka hastily folded her work and, snatching a broken piece of mirror from under her pillow, arranged the curls on her forehead, gave a touch of rouge to her lips, and ran downstairs.

"Citizen Korf! Visitors!"

I was left waiting. I could not sit still, so I went out into the yard and strolled toward the gate.

The prostitute Zinka, wearing a wreath from one of the graves on her head, was dancing and singing a bawdy song. Here and there women were sitting on the graves, drinking tea and talking in low tones. In a far corner, on the round top of a low tomb, the baroness was serving coffee to a friend who came every Sunday. They sat prim and erect at their strange table and talked French.

Suddenly Zinka made a dash for the kitchen, swinging her kettle and bumping into everyone on the way.

"Crazy devil!" a woman shouted. "Can't you see?"

"Mother, mother has come to visit me!" Zinka called back in apology.

The fat little girl we called "Dumpling" was trailing wearily up and down the path, cracking maple leaves with her lips.

"Waiting for your mother?" I asked.

"Mm! Ye! But she won't come, she's always sick."

"Citizen Tolstoy! Someone is asking for you." That meant friends or relatives, and baskets of provisions, enough for a whole week. I hurried to the gate, smiling in anticipation.

Sometimes my sister Tania came. Like the baroness, she picked up her skirts for fear of being soiled. There was horror in her eyes, and she turned away in disgust from the curses and songs of the prostitutes, their bright-colored rags and painted faces. One-eyed Dunka, imitating Zinka, tore a wreath off a tomb and played about with it, cursing amiably, contorting her body, and making faces. Tania seemed a creature from a different world; and, feeling with her, I suffered more than ever. I was actually relieved when she left. The shameless way these women had of eavesdropping and the sordid atmosphere of the place spoiled her visits. Yet, more than anything else, her coming brought me close to the life that was going on "out there."

No sooner was Sunday over than everyone began looking forward to the next Sunday; and by Saturday our excitement had risen to such a pitch that we could not sleep. Anna Fedorovna, Dunia, and the governor's daughter did not share in even this pleasure. They had no friends in the city.

"ALL criminals to work!"[1]

Some of us—political prisoners—joined the party. It was already getting dark. The gates in the high monastery walls stood wide open. Flat cars brought up wood and it was unloaded outside. Beyond the track a line of soldiers was stationed.

The beams we were to carry were so heavy that two women could hardly drag one the five hundred yards to the prison yard. George was the only laborer who enjoyed herself. Joking, swearing, and making fun of her companions, she tossed a beam on to her shoulder and jogged off. I did not like to ask for help, so I took one by myself. It was too heavy, one end went down, and I had to stop. Someone bumped into me.

"Be careful!" I shouted.

"Damn you! Why are you stopping? Keep out of the way!" a voice behind me cried.

I dropped my beam and looked back. There was a tall slender girl, also carrying a beam. I went back and took one end of it from her. We carried it together, and when we unloaded it and stopped to rest she asked me who I was.

---

[1] At that time, political prisoners were not obliged to do physical labor. Most of them worked in the office or the prison theater. Today they are usually sent to the northern lumber camps.

"Let's work together," I said. "They're too heavy for one of us alone."

It seemed to me that she winked at me strangely, as if in mockery. I could not see well in the dark, but when she turned her face toward the street lamp, I saw that her eye was white.

"Did I hurt you?" she asked suddenly.

"Not at all."

"Are you one of the political crowd?"

"Yes."

"I thought so. Well, then, why are you working? You don't have to. You people are queer."

"What's your name?"

"Dunka. They call me One-eyed Dunka."

We worked together all the evening.

The moon was high, sailing above fast-moving white clouds. It would disappear for a moment, leaving the sky dark and leaden. And then suddenly it would reappear and pour a mysterious silver-green light on the world. The dirt, misery, and weariness of the faces about us were transformed. Everything seemed purified by this magic light. Here and there the dark line of the monastery walls gleamed white, and the majestic domes of the churches were full of mysterious beauty.

We sat on a log and rested, and watched the clouds.

"You bitches! Daughters of . . .! I'll teach you to sit here and enjoy yourselves when the others are working."

We had not noticed the guard approaching.

XXVII

THE ROMANOVSKY VAULT

WITH the help of Anna Fedorovna and one of the prisoners who was a teacher, I started a school for the illiterate prisoners. The commandant approved. He even let me go to the Commissariat of Education to get textbooks. Our program was not ambitious. We only tried to teach reading, writing, and arithmetic. I persuaded some writers and professors to lecture to the whole camp on literature, economics, and other subjects.

In addition to concerts by outside artists, we had a camp chorus which sang Russian and gypsy songs. We were invited to sing in other prisons, and soon made our camp famous. Well disguised in peasant costume and cosmetics so that I would not be recognized, I conducted and played the guitar.

WE had to find out how many students we would have in our classes. The commandant told us we could write down the names of those who were illiterate during the evening count of prisoners which took place in the yard. The women had to line up like soldiers, and the commandant, accompanied by his assistant and guards, would walk along the line, checking those who were present.

"Stepanova!"

"Yes."

"Literate?"

"No."

"Ilvovskaya!"

"Here."

"Literate?"

"Yes, finished Class B in high school."

"Kurochkina!"

One of the women was talking to her neighbor and did not hear.

"Take her to the cellar!"

"But what for, Comrade Commandant? What have I done?"

"Shut up! Put her in the cellar!"

"You have no right to put me in the cellar! I've done nothing! How dare you?"

"I'll show you how I dare! Take her to the Romanovsky vault!"

The guards seized Kurochkina and dragged her off, wriggling and screaming. The checking went on.

"Ivanova!"

"Yes."

"Kolpikova!"

"Yes."

With a heavy heart I returned to my cell. Very soon two women rushed in.

"Anna Fedorovna! Come! Kurochkina is having a fit."

We ran downstairs and out to the cemetery. The tomb of the Romanovs was a deep vault without windows, damp and completely dark. Stone steps led down to it, and an enormous padlock hung on the door. We could just hear a dull thumping inside.

"It's another of her epileptic fits," one of the women said. "She may beat herself to death on that stone floor."

"Come on to the commandant!" said Anna Fedorovna. "Perhaps he'll listen." We raced to the office.

"Comrade Commandant!" Anna Fedorovna gasped. "Please have Kurochkina taken to the dispensary, she's having an epileptic fit."

Pretending that he did not hear, the commandant went on speaking to his assistant.

"Comrade Commandant, she will bruise herself on the stone floor, she may kill herself."

"Don't stick your nose into things that don't concern you, Anna Fedorovna."

"It does concern us!" I cried. "If you don't let the woman out, you will be held responsible!"

The commandant turned on me.

"Shut up, I know what I am doing. If you don't hold your tongue, you'll join the hussy in the cellar!"

"I don't care, but you will be reported to the Executive Committee and the party."

The commandant clenched his fists and took a step toward me. Then he stopped short, turned, and left the room.

Kurochkina was unconscious when they took her out of the vault. Her body was twisted by convulsions, her mouth was full of foam, and there was a rattle in her throat. Instead of taking her to the dispensary, they threw her into another cell, locked the door, and left her.

NADIA was only seventeen, but she looked like an old woman. She never laughed and never smiled. I often found her sitting on a tomb with her eyes strangely fixed on one spot.

"Nadia!"

She would look up without seeing me, like someone who is plunged in painful, unhealthy dreams.

"Nadia—again?" the governor's daughter asked her. "You are letting yourself go to pieces!"

Nadia's head drooped.

"I don't care. I don't suffer when I take it."

The governor's daughter bent down and whispered something in her ear. The girl sprang to her feet, pushing her aside.

"Never speak to me about her! Never, do you understand? She would never forgive . . . It's no use! I don't care!"

She laughed and cried, her eyes burned, and bright red spots glowed in her cheeks.

"Quietly, quietly," the governor's daughter said. "Come and lie down in my room."

"You invite me—you, a lady! Do you know who I am?" she suddenly turned to me.

"Stop it, Nadia! Stop it!"

"Ah! Afraid I'll say the word. You are too respectable to hear it, are you?"

"Come away. She will calm down better alone," the governor's daughter said mournfully. "Poor creature!"

"Go to the devil! Saints! Respectable people! Don't come near me again, you red-haired hypocrite!"

All the evening I could not forget the unnaturally bright eyes and hysterical laughter of the drug-intoxicated girl.

Once Nadia told us her story. I do not know whether it was true. It was like many others we had heard, but it was exceptionally vivid.

She had lived with her parents in the territory of the Whites near the Western frontier. Her people were farmers. In winter Nadia went to school, in summer she helped on the farm. Once, without knowing it, she crossed the frontier. Some Red soldiers arrested her and took her to a small town to prison. She was suspected of being a spy. For several days she was kept locked up. The commandant was kind to her, gave her a good room and food, joked with her, and at last promised to let her out on certain conditions. Sensing more than understanding what he wanted, for she was only sixteen, she refused. He violated her and, furious at her resistance, threw her again into the prison. She was passed from one guard to another. To get rid of her the commandant sent her to Moscow, where she was very ill. In a hospital there, a woman taught her the use of drugs.

THE roly-poly little girl called "Dumpling" could not have been more than fifteen. Her face was childlike, and her name suited her wonderfully: she really reminded one of a well-baked apple dumpling.

The prisoners liked her, but always made fun of her good humoredly.

"Hallo, Dumpling! Tell us why they put you in prison."

She only smiled.

"Tell me, Dumpling, I don't know about it."

"I was imprisoned for dumplings!" the girl said, lowering her small blue eyes.

"What do you mean—'for dumplings'?"

At first she blushed and would not talk. But finally, seeing that I was not making fun of her, she told me.

Her mother baked dumplings, and she took them to market. They did not have a license for selling—it cost too much. So she had to be on the watch for the police all the time. Every now and then there would be an alarm, and everyone would pick up his goods and scamper in different directions—into side streets or people's yards.

"Well," Dumpling said, "once I got caught. They took me to the police station, and they ate all my dumplings, the beasts. They were still warm, mother had just taken them out of the oven. They ate every one."

Dumpling sighed and gulped.

"Well, they put me in prison. That's all."

"Dumpling," one-eyed Dunka teased, "that was the first time that you were in prison. Why did they take you the second time? Tell the lady all about that!"

"Leave me alone!"

"Tell me, Dumpling," I said, "I won't laugh at you."

Suddenly the childish face puckered into a funny grimace, the corners of the rosy mouth went down, and Dumpling burst out crying.

"LITTLE madam! Will you let me have a cigarette?"

"Certainly. Are you Ilvovskaya?"

"No—well, yes, I am. You see, I've changed my name so often I forget it sometimes."

"Why do you change it?"

"Well, you have to in my profession. If you are working as Vasilieva and you are caught and put in prison, you get released as Vladimirova, and the next time . . ."

"Oh, the sneak," George interrupted. "You don't mean to say you have a profession?"

"Don't bite me, madam. I'm not talking to you, am I? Picking pockets is a profession. And sometimes we have two jobs at a time. You should see what boys I pick up: you'd be crazy with envy. I had an apartment to myself once. Which name do you think is the best, madam—Vasilieva or Ilvovskaya?"

"Well, I can't say. Why are you imprisoned?"

"Oh, for just a trifle! A gold watch and chain. Oh, little madam, I was so foolish! You won't believe it, but I fell in love. An Armenian. Such a darling! Eyes like fire, gold studs and an English suit. Such style. I fell in love. And he?—there was nothing he wouldn't do for me. But my damned profession spoiled it all. It happened in a hotel. He fell asleep, but I was wide awake, and his gold watch and chain simply tormented me. I would lie in bed, and every so often I would raise myself on my elbow and look at them. The ticking of the watch just tortured me, and the gold chain looked so beautiful on the night table, I couldn't bear it. I got up quietly, dressed, and grabbed the watch and chain. But before I got to the door he had me by the arm. Caught. Little madam, may I have another cigarette?"

Ilvovskaya lit it and broke into a song that was popular in the camp:

> I am sitting on a barrel,
> And a mouse is underneath.
> When the Whites are on the barrel
> The Reds will be beneath.

"She's not afraid of anything!" Anna Fedorovna said, shaking her head.

"Ragpicker!" George muttered between her teeth.

XXVIII

AUNT LIZA

I NEVER saw anyone who seemed less like a convict than Aunt Liza. She was a peasant woman who could hardly read and write, yet everybody respected her. She was poor, she did not look like a counterrevolutionary, and I often wondered what she was imprisoned for. One day I asked her.

"For distilling!" she said simply.

"What? You don't mean you were making vodka?" I exclaimed, my mental picture of the good old woman suddenly altering.

"God bless you, no! Our religion doesn't allow it. We don't drink, don't smoke, and we must remain pure in every sense. I wouldn't touch such filthy stuff as vodka!"

"Well, then, how did you happen to get in prison?"

"My neighbor was making brandy when the police came. She got frightened and took the kettle out of her cellar and threw it into my barn. The police found it, and took me to prison and kept me six months, with no examination and no trial. I wish there would be a trial at the court of justice; I could certainly prove that I am innocent. Well, there's nothing to be done. The spirit of God is everywhere, and after all, it is His holy will."

Every Sunday morning a girl of twelve came to Aunt Liza's cell carrying a bundle. Nobody else was allowed to entertain visitors in her cell, but the guards liked Aunt Liza and made exceptions for her.

"She is an adopted child of ours," Aunt Liza explained, stroking the girl's hair, "the twelfth orphan that we are bringing up. All the others are grown up and have jobs now. Four of them are married."

I begged her to tell me about her life.

"Well, what shall I tell you?" she asked. "I am not much of a story teller. My people were sectarians, and we took the vow of chastity. We did not like the idea of mutilating ourselves. We simply promised to lead a sinless life. Well, God helped me."

"Was it hard for you, Aunt Liza?"

"No . . . I was tempted only once . . . I got fond of a lad. Oh, how he begged me to marry him, and when I refused, he cursed and mocked at me. The devil is strong! I could not sleep or eat; they thought I would die. It looked like consumption. Then after a while it all passed away, and now I can see clearly that it was nothing but foolishness, weakness. Well, my sister couldn't bear it. She fell. Once when she came home she cried her eyes out and told me she was pregnant. What was to be done? Her seducer abandoned her. A little girl was born, but she lived only a week and died. And then we promised, my sister and I, that we would pray and spend our lives bringing up orphan girls in memory of our little girl that died, to expiate my sister's sin."

"How do you live?"

"Simply enough. We have a small house, a knitting machine, three goats, about ten laying hens. We get along. We don't need very much."

Aunt Liza had the spirit of the Russian peasant that my father worshiped all his life. I liked everything about her: her dark eyes that were sometimes red from her laborious reading of the Bible; her thin bony cheeks; full, dark cotton dress; the kerchief tied under her chin; her rough shoes and stockings. She did not talk much, and never criticized anyone; yet the criminals and prostitutes never swore in her presence.

A month after I came to the prison, Aunt Liza was set free.

"I want to say goodbye to Aunt Liza!" George roared, bursting into our cell.

"Aunt Liza, take some bread!"

"May I carry your things to the gate for you?"

Everybody was happy. The guards were smiling, too.

"How lonely we shall be without you, dear little pigeon!" the governor's daughter said, wiping a tear off her cheek. "But I am so happy, so happy for you!"

"I shall come and see you on Sunday," Aunt Liza promised.

The heavy gate opened. Aunt Liza, with a bag on her back and a basket in her hand, bowed to the crowd of women who had come to see her off, and saying "God bless you!" walked slowly away.

XXIX

A RED ARMY SOLDIER

I HAD a toothache. At the dispensary they gave me aspirin and put iodine on the gum, but the pain continued. I went to the commandant and asked to be allowed to go to the dentist.

"I have nothing against your going," he said. "There are three more prisoners who want to go, but I don't know whether there are guards to take you."

"Kuzia is free," his assistant said.

"All right then, let Kuzia take them."

We had to go to another camp about two miles away, where there was a dentist. We waited in the office for the guard.

"Come on," Kuzia called, entering.

I stared in amazement. Kuzia was a woman!

"Don't go so fast," she cried, for we started off at a good speed, glad to have exercise.

"Can't you keep up with us?" a woman with a red shawl on her head retorted.

"Of course she can't," another one said mockingly. "Don't you see, she's tangled up in her cape. Kuzia! take care, don't lose your boots!"

I looked back at Kuzia. She was a lamentable creature. Her thin little face was nearly lost in her cap, her soldier's cape swept the ground and her boots were so big that she had to drag her feet. A heavy gun lay on her slender shoulder and a great pistol hung at her belt. She looked about sixteen.

"Kuzia," I said, "what if we try to run away?"

"I'll catch you!"

"How can you catch us? We're four to your one. We'll go in different directions and you'll never be able to get us."

"If I catch one of you, that'll be enough. I can't be responsible for all of you."

"Oh, you tin soldier, why should you be responsible?"—the

woman in the red shawl said. "You have a revolver. One, two, three, four—you'll shoot us and then you won't have to answer for us . . ."

"Oh, the revolver isn't loaded. But you won't do such a thing," the girl said peevishly. "Why should you run away? You wouldn't be so cruel to me."

And suddenly she shouted: "Don't you hear my orders? Go slower! . . . Beasts!"

XXX

THE COMMANDANT

EVERY morning Anna Fedorovna received our day's ration—sugar and butter and half a pound of bread for
each of us. She spread pieces of newspaper on the table
and cut the yellow butter, soiled with fingerprints, into tiny
shares. Then she distributed a teaspoonful of sugar to each of
us. The soup that was given us for dinner was usually made
out of potato skins; as the potatoes had been frozen and it was
difficult to wash them, there was always plenty of dirt in it. We
had to restrain our appetites until the dirt settled to the bottom.
Millet cereal was our second dish. Sometimes we had the same
cereal again for supper; and sometimes dry salted fish, so dry
that I would beat it furiously against the gravestones for fifteen
minutes until it got soft and the bright orange roe tumbled out.

The prisoners were always hungry and always trading with
each other.

"Hallo, Dumpling!" someone would shout. "George is trading bread for cigarettes!" and the girl would run to George's
cell to get bread.

In our cell only the Armenian woman, imprisoned for speculating in jewelry, and I received food from outside. According
to prison ethics, the food we got had to be divided among all
the prisoners in the cell. Cigarettes alone were considered private property. About once a month, sugar, sunflower oil, and
cigarettes were sent us by the Red Cross. Then we had a party.
We lighted the fire, soaked bread in oil, fried it, and had tea
with plenty of sugar. It was cozy in our small cell around the
blue-tiled fireplace. Sometimes we even forgot we were in
prison.

The governor's daughter never joined these parties.

"Come and have some roast beef!" we would call to her.

"Thank you, I am not hungry," she invariably answered.

Every morning, Nadia or someone else was seen coming out

of her room with a bottle of oil or a package of something in her hand. She even gave her day's portion of butter to Dunia or the baroness.

"You are killing yourself," Anna Fedorovna would say. "It isn't right!"

"I do not like butter," she would answer with her sweet smile, "I feel better without it."

It was rumored that most of our food was taken by the administration of the camp. The prisoners were indignant, but did not dare say anything.

"How much do the commandant and his helpers get?" I once asked Anna Fedorovna.

"They're not supposed to get any of our food," she replied. "They have their own."

"Well, why doesn't anyone protest?"

She only gestured hopelessly.

But when for dinner we got the same potato soup and cereal—

"I am going to the commandant," I said. "I can't stand seeing the prisoners starve!"

"It's no use, Alexandra Lvovna, I assure you."

But I was roused and I picked up my dishes and marched off. The commandant was sitting at his desk, frowning over a paper he held in his hand.

"Comrade Commandant! Look at what they are feeding us!"

"W H A T ?"

"Are potato peelings and cereal without butter the food that the Soviet Government provides for the prisoners?"

"What is the matter with you, Citizen Tolstoy? Are you becoming insubordinate?"

"I want the prisoners to get what is due them!"

His broad ugly face suddenly became purple, and an enormous fist slammed on the table.

"Shut up! Hallo, guard! Write this down: 'Citizen Tolstoy is to be on duty in the kitchen the twenty-fifth and twenty-sixth of December!'"

It was dark when I woke on Christmas day and went to the

kitchen. "Uncle Misha," the only monk left in the monastery, went with rattling keys to the storeroom to get provisions, and the cooks began dividing the food into two parts.

"What are you doing that for?" I asked.

"Half is for the commandant and his helpers."

"Not a bit of it!" I said. "All this food must be given to the prisoners!"

"You don't mean to say that you are not going to share it with the . . . ?"

"I mean what I say. The commandant and his helpers have no right to it, and won't get it, that's all!"

The prisoners had a good Christmas dinner. But the commandant was furious.

"He will never forgive you," Anna Fedorovna said. "If he doesn't punish you now, he'll revenge himself later."

I knew that my position would become thoroughly unpleasant. The commandant had been kind to me before, and occasionally allowed me to go to town, once to the Commissariat of Education to get a magic lantern for the lectures, two or three times to the dentist. He had approved of my work with the school and lectures, and sent in somewhat embroidered reports about the educational work in his camp. Now everything would change.

Nothing of mine was safe henceforth. I sent my diary home to some friends once a week in an empty bottle, and during the other six days, kept the manuscript in the stove under a loose tile.

The dressmaker Mania, who had recently been put in our cell, asked me what I was writing.

"A novel!" I answered, "and you're in it, Mania!"

We did not trust Mania very far. She was friendly with the commandant's wife and often visited her.

"Mania, what is this?" exclaimed the Armenian, when Mania once brought out a beautiful heavy lilac velvet and spread it on her bed.

"This is to be a dress for the commandant's wife," she said.

"He's got plenty of those wives," one of the women said, as

she leaned forward to see the material. "Is this new stuff or used?"

"Where did he get it from?" asked the Armenian.

"Leave me alone! It isn't any of your business, is it? I'll have to tell the commandant if you go on poking your nose in things that don't concern you!"

The women were silent, but I could see that their curiosity—especially the Armenian's—was not satisfied.

Soon Mania took away the velvet dress and brought a new material that was even more beautiful. It was heavy white silk with gold brocade. No questions were asked. But one day, as I was talking to Anna Fedorovna, the Armenian rushed into the room. "Good God!" she whispered. "She is making dresses out of the bishop's robes! Look at this!"

On the floor, among the odds and ends, she had found a piece of silk with a cross embroidered in gold.

"Anna Fedorovna," I asked when we were alone, "did you know that the commandant is robbing the monastery?"

"Yes, I knew it long ago. But what is to be done? If it isn't robbed today, it will be tomorrow. Not long since the commandant sold a gold cross that weighed more than five pounds. He has stolen a lot of things, and his predecessors used their time well. I don't think there's much left now but the bishop's robes."

"But weren't the things registered?"

"I don't know. I am trying not to think about it. It is two years since I was transferred here from Butyrki. I've seen plenty of people getting excited as you are, trying to change things, fighting with the administration. It's no use. This commandant seems to you the worst beast you could find. Well, he may be; but we know him, and we know how to deal with him. If he is dismissed, they may send somebody a lot worse."

Mania may have reported that I was writing something, or she may have missed the piece of material with the gold cross. Or the commandant may have been trying to find a way of getting even. At all events, in the middle of the night, heavy footsteps sounded on the stairs and the commandant with several guards entered to search our cell. They hardly looked at my companions' things, but they neglected nothing of mine. They pulled my bedding to pieces and tore off the pillow cases. The commandant became more and more irritated.

"Tear up the floor!" he ordered.

They searched for about two hours but found nothing. My manuscript and the bishop's cross lay safe under the old white tile with the blue edges in the stove.

XXXI

THE INSPECTOR

A STRANGE creature came into the room. For a moment I could not tell whether it was a boy or a woman. Short curly hair, black eyes shining like ripe olives, a small nose, a red blouse, black leather jacket, short black skirt, and high boots. The Russian costume somehow did not harmonize with the strikingly Jewish face. The girl came in followed by the commandant, his assistant, and a woman in European dress.

"It's the Workers' and Peasants' Inspection!" Anna Fedorovna whispered.

"Is the bedding your own?" the little Jewess asked. She seemed to be the most important member of the commission.

"Our own," Anna Fedorovna answered.

"How often do you change your sheets and pillow cases?"

The question made me laugh.

"Why are you laughing?" She turned on me sharply. "Let me see!" and she pulled down the blankets on my bed and examined the sheets.

"They are clean."

"These are political prisoners," the commandant said.

"Why didn't you say so before? Your family name?" she asked me.

"Tolstoy."

"Oh! I'd like to speak to you. I'll see you later."

The inspector and her escort left the room, and I went to the office where I had to take a count of the prisoners for a national census. No sooner did we begin the work than the little inspector came again with her followers, and in the same busy, fussy way continued her questioning.

Then with a grand gesture of her tiny hand, she dismissed the commandant and his helpers: "Please leave us, comrades. I want to have a private talk with the prisoners."

"Well," she said, when the others left the room, "I am the representative of the Workers' and Peasants' Inspection, and also a member of the Women's Department of the Communist party. Our government is anxious that citizens, workers, and peasants who did wrong under the influence and tyranny of the tsarist *régime* shall not be punished in our prisons, but shall have a chance to improve. That is why the government is trying to organize educational institutions to spread the ideas of our Communist party among the prisoners, so that they can be educated in the true spirit of socialism. Comrades, you must all be with us! You must all help us to build up our socialistic country! As soon as you get free, every one of you must join the ranks of the proletariat, which is fighting for the freedom and happiness of the working class! Who is doing educational work in the camp?"

Silence.

"Who is working with the illiterates?"

"I am."

"Comrade Tolstoy?"

"Yes."

"And how are you helping Communist propaganda?"

"I am not helping it."

"Why not?"

"Because I do not approve of it."

"I see. That is interesting. I shall talk to you afterwards. And now, comrades, please tell me how you are living here. How are you fed? Are you given clothes? Do you get enough wood for your stoves?"

The prisoners were silent.

"Comrades, I am asking you: are there any complaints about the food? How does the commandant behave toward you?"

"What is the use of asking all those questions?" I asked irritably. "Don't you understand that if we are silent, it is not because we have nothing to complain of? Every one of us knows that if we tell you the truth we will be punished as soon as you leave the camp: thrown into the cellar or worked to the bone!"

"Comrades!" the little inspector exclaimed, "Comrade Tolstoy is not right. I will answer for your safety!" and she planted her hand on her chest. "Please tell me everything. Don't be afraid!"

And again the prisoners were silent.

"Well!"

"Let me ask you a question," I said. "How can we say anything when we do not know what is due us? We only know that they are feeding us frozen potato peelings, that we haven't got enough bread, that we are given old dirty clothes that are good for nothing . . . but we don't know what we ought to have!"

"Is this all true?" the inspector asked.

"Of course it's true," one of the prisoners said. "We never get the food that is due us, the commandant punishes us for no reason at all . . . we don't get our share of sugar . . ."

"I see. Then why were you silent, comrades? Why didn't you speak up at once? Haven't you waked up yet?"

The inspection was over. The inspector went away. The prisoners waited anxiously. Then another inspection consisting of two men and a woman came. They visited the kitchen, questioned the prisoners, made notes. The little Jewess returned frequently.

"Comrade Tolstoy," she said once, "would you like to go to the theater? I'll tell the commandant to let you."

"No, thank you."

"Why not?"

"No, thank you, I will not go."

Sometimes she would talk politics to me, repeating the stereotyped words about the Soviet paradise, the awakening of the consciousness of the proletariat, the world revolution. I had heard those speeches so many times, but she wanted to talk and was glad when I argued with her.

"Socialism is impossible in Russia," I said once. "First of all, because the people are not educated enough, and second because socialism can be instilled only when the working class realize its advantages. But they will never realize; for them there are only disadvantages . . ."

This was enough to make the Communist speak for hours. I was bored with her talk.

Once we advised Dunia to write a petition to the Workers' and Peasants' Inspection and give it to the inspector. We were all sorry for this mild, harmless creature who was suffering for no reason. The petition was written. Instead of a signature Dunia put a shaky cross under it, and somebody signed it for her.

"Why were you arrested?" the Communist asked as she looked over the petition.

"How do I know?"

"Where did you live?"

"Near the frontier. My parents were on the side of the Reds, and I was with relatives on the other side. Well, I decided to go to the Reds . . ."

"Why did you go?"

"Well, I thought it would be better with the Reds . . ."

"Don't be so silly next time, Dunia," I said. "You have been punished for it."

"You are wicked," the little Communist said, threatening me with a dirty little finger. And to Dunia:

"All right then. Give me your petition, Comrade Dunia, and we shall see what we can do."

"Thank you, dear lady!"

"I am not a lady. I'm your comrade. Are you going to school, Comrade Dunia?"

"Yes, I am."

"Fine! When you get out of prison, you will be a conscientious, literate citizen. Perhaps we shall fight together for the workers and the peasants, and, who knows, you may yet become a commissar . . ."

Dunia blinked her gray eyes uncomprehendingly and smiled. She was glad that the Communist had taken her petition.

My nerves were on edge. I could not restrain myself.

"Such people as Dunia will never become commissars," I said.

"Why?"

"She is too honest."

"What do you mean?"

"Oh, nothing in particular. But I think that the only place for honest people nowadays is in prisons and camps. The power is in the hands of comrades who were formerly the Tsar's guards, who shot their forefingers off to get out of the war, and are . . ."

"Will you please continue."

". . . are robbing our ancient Russian treasures. You are a baby. You don't know. You say you are a representative of the workers and the peasants. Where have you seen the peasants? Out of a train window?"

"You are insulting me, Comrade Tolstoy. I am a bench worker myself."

I went into the next room, closed the door, and got the gold cross from under the tile.

"There! These are your honest workers from the ranks of the proletariat!" I exclaimed, throwing the piece of silk on the table. "Did you ever see bishops' robes? This is what the commandant makes the dresses for his women of. He robs the sacristy, he robs the prisoners, he starves them, tortures them . . ."

"Give that to me!" the little Jewess exclaimed, and, seizing the gold cross, she disappeared.

The commandant was dismissed. I felt more secure. But Anna Fedorovna was right. Conditions did not improve.

XXXII

THE THEATER

"GET up, Alexandra Lvovna!"

"Ugh! Where? Why?"

I opened my eyes and saw soldiers' gray coats. Anna Fedorovna was shaking me by the shoulder.

"I don't know why," she said. "We are all ordered to go to the theater. The camp is surrounded by soldiers!"

"What is going on in the theater at this time of night?" I muttered. "I don't want to go to the theater!"

"No one's asking if you want to go or not. Get up!" the soldiers ordered as they left the room.

"A search!" Anna Fedorovna whispered.

I jumped out of bed.

"Anna Fedorovna! What shall we do with our things? And our money, shall we take it with us?"

"Yes, we might as well. They'll take it if you leave it here, anyhow."

"Will they search here, too?"

"Of course. They're taking us to the theater because they don't want us in their way."

"The manuscript," I thought, "what shall I do with it? Burn it? No, let it stay where it is. They won't find it."

Out in the yard, under the high trees, soldiers in sharp-pointed helmets were moving among the tombs with lighted torches. Motorcycles were roaring, racing their engines, and prisoners in small groups hurried toward the theater. I moved in a sort of stupor. It seemed to me that I had never seen this place before; these trees throwing fantastic shadows on the ground, huge stones, enormous white walls . . . It might be Hell.

The theater was packed. There were three people on the stage: a woman, our new commandant, and another man who turned out to be from the Cheka. For two hours we sat shivering with cold and fear. Then they began calling out the prisoners. It was morning when my turn came.

"Tolstoy!"

I made my way through the crowd toward the stage. The woman questioned me: When was I arrested? Why? What was my chief occupation? Had I any money? She took my purse away and with quick movements, showing how used she was to it, moved her hands over my body, hair, stockings, and turned out the pockets of my coat. At every movement she made I shivered with disgust, and I had to keep myself from pushing her away.

I joined my friends on the way out. We thought we could at last go to our cell and sleep, but instead we were taken to the isolation ward for syphilitics. There were no beds here, only wooden cots. The room was dirty. Prisoners were sitting on the pallets and on the floor; those who were afraid of the disease were standing. It was crowded and close, but more and more prisoners were brought from the theater. Not until about nine o'clock were we allowed to go back to our cell. Everything had been upset, boxes emptied and their contents thrown all over the room. The beds had been pulled to pieces. I looked under the tile: my manuscript was there.

Later I went to the theater. It was a strange sight. The floor was littered with bits of paper. The prisoners, afraid of the Cheka, had torn up all their letters.

Our money was never given back.

"Why didn't you give it to me?" George said. "I could have saved it for you!"

"How?"

"Oh, how? That's a professional secret."

XXXIII

TYPIST

TWO men came from the Transportation Department of the Commissariat of Food Supplies. A few of us were summoned to the office and inquiries were made about our occupations. It had never occurred to me before that I really had no profession at all. What were my occupations? Editorial work? Farming?

"Say something!" the Armenian whispered. "They'll take us out of here!"

"Typist!" I exclaimed.

The men made notes and went away, and we forgot all about them, as we forgot many other visits. But in about a week or two, we were again called into the office.

"Pack your things!"

I was ready in ten minutes and said embarrassed goodbyes to my companions, feeling both sorry to leave them and glad to go. A big green truck was standing by the gate of the monastery, and a pleasant-looking young man invited us to climb in. As the truck bumped through the streets of Moscow, I could not help smiling stupidly to myself. Four months in the camp, and now—freedom!

I was taken to a dirty little office full of tobacco smoke, and given an old Underwood typewriter, and a number of papers to copy. I had never typed anything but father's manuscripts before. These official forms were strange to me and nobody bothered to explain them.

"What are you doing?" one of the men exclaimed, when I brought him a copy of a paper written by the boss. I had corrected the spelling but had left the text, which was barely intelligible, as it was. "You can't do it that way! You've got to catch his drift and write it your own way. He'll sign it."

In a few days I learned how to do it. The director was pleased. But I hated my work, especially the accounts. Figures bored me and I never could type them in straight columns. Soon papers were given to me for typing, not only from our department, but from others, too. One paper followed another. The faster I typed, the more work was given to me. They did not even bother to write out the contents, but simply shouted to me across the room:

"Comrade Tolstoy! Department of Supplies: a reprimand for delaying . . ."

"All right!"

I could not understand why the other typists worked quietly till four o'clock, calmly put away their work and went home, while I worked every day until seven and was always tormented by the thought that I had not finished everything that was given me.

"Did you ever have a job before?" the Armenian asked me.

"No, never."

"I thought so. You don't know how to do it. When they bring you something to copy, you must say that you have no time for it, that you have several urgent papers to copy and so on. But if you just accept all the typing that is given you, they'll work you to death!"

We did not receive wages for our work, but we did get dinner and food shares.

After work, I could go home, and see relatives and friends. Only theaters, concerts, and meetings were forbidden. But I could not resist going to a meeting held in my father's honor, at which Bulgakov, his last secretary, spoke against capital punishment. Bulgakov was not afraid to voice his thoughts publicly. His best speech was on November 20, 1920. The Communists tried to shout him down, and he told them sternly: "You have lost the habit of listening to free speech!" His immediate arrest was desired, but it was not carried out. In March, 1923, he was exiled.

I do not remember who reported that I had attended a meeting; but the news got into the papers. A few days later I was again arrested and taken back to camp.

The prosecutor, Krylenko, was said to be furious. In any case, an order was given to keep me under strict surveillance.

XXXIV

THE BARONESS AND THE PEASANTS

IN the two months that I had been free everything seemed to have changed in the camp. The governor's daughter and the baroness had been taken to another prison, and there were a lot of new prisoners. I was put in a different cell with Anna Fedorovna and some others. Now everybody was fascinated by the famous Baroness Von Stein—"Sonka of the Golden Hand," as she was nicknamed—a clever swindler and thief. As soon as I arrived all the prisoners began praising her and her remarkable fortune telling. George was the only one who was skeptical.

"Filthy scoundrel!" she said, "stealing from her own! That is the last thing a decent thief will do. She stole Nadia's gold bracelet, the only thing the girl had!"

Even political prisoners went to the baroness to have their fortunes told.

"She doesn't look like a dishonest person," they said. "She is so gracious and well dressed, she speaks several languages— and she tells your fortune wonderfully!"

"*Mademoiselle la comtesse! Charmée de vous voir!*"

A tall gray-headed lady in a black silk dress stood in the doorway.

I was silent.

"I am so happy to meet you, Countess," she went on in English, and, as I said nothing, she changed to German:

"*Ich habe Ihres Vaters Bücher gelesen!*"

She talked for at least three minutes, skipping from one language to another, smiling pleasantly.

"Will you allow me to tell your fortune?"

"No, thank you," I said at last. "I do not make acquaintances in prison."

She muttered something in French and, seeing that there was

no use wasting time with such a rude person, she turned to my companions.

Very little happened during my second stay at the camp. I was depressed. I did not even continue to write my diary. Life was dull, and days and persons all alike.

Meanwhile people were trying to get me out of prison.

"Why should you stay in prison?" the little Jewess asked. "You can work for us, for the working class. And you will be much more useful out of prison!"

She got an appointment for me with an important member of the party, Comrade Kollontay, and in great excitement arranged a pass for me to appear before the Central Party Committee.

I did not expect to find Comrade Kollontay so pleasant. She was ladylike, cultured in manner, and apparently clever. I do not know what impression I made on her, but in about ten days the little Jewess rushed into my cell:

"Comrade Tolstoy! Comrade Tolstoy! I have news for you! Shall I tell?"

"Well, what is it?"

"All the members of the Central Party Committee but one have voted for your freedom, and it has been decided to plead your cause before the Central Executive Committee."

She laughed, jumped and skipped all over the cell, and finally turned a somersault.

The peasants, too, were pleading my cause. Three representatives from Yasnaia Poliana and the two neighboring villages went to the President of the Central Executive Committee, Kalinin. I wanted to see them, as well as my sister, who was also in Moscow, but the commandant would not let me out.

"Please let me go, Comrade Commandant!" I begged him. "I will be back in a few hours!"

He looked at me attentively. "Impossible! Your face is too noticeable . . . one can recognize it among thousands . . . with those glasses. No, it's impossible!"

He was good-natured, this new commandant, who wore

glasses himself and tried to look like an intellectual. But he was afraid of disobeying orders.

I did not answer and left the room.

Half an hour later I was back again, dressed in Dunia's wide flounced skirt, her peasant blouse, and a large red shawl. I had taken my glasses off, plucked and darkened my eyebrows, and painted my cheeks and lips.

"What do you want here?" the commandant asked sharply when I approached his desk.

"Of your kindness, father, allow me to say . . ."

"Where do you come from? Who are you?"

"Don't you recognize me, Comrade Commandant?" I said in my own voice.

"Damn it, it's you, Comrade Tolstoy! Well, well! I would never have recognized you. It seems there is nothing to be done! I don't think Prosecutor Krylenko himself would recognize you in those clothes. I will let you go on two conditions: first, that you are back at ten o'clock; and second, that you keep your glasses off. They change your face a good deal."

"All right. Thank you!"

It was already dark when I started. I had to go by the lonely quays along the Moscow River. Suddenly I heard footsteps behind me and a soldier overtook me.

"Let's get acquainted," he said.

I stopped short, and putting my glasses on my nose, looked at him sternly.

"You do not know with whom you are speaking, comrade," I said. "Do you want to go to the police?"

"Excuse me, comrade," he said, saluting.

"WHAT does the masquerade mean?" my sister asked when I got home.

"Let me wash the paint off and then I'll tell you."

The peasant representatives had brought with them a petition to Kalinin, signed by the peasants of three villages: Yasnaia Poliana, Grumond, and Teliatinki.

We all had tea in my room, with real homemade black

bread. The peasants talked business. They did not use sentimental words of pity or compassion. Only, when we finished
our tea, the youngest of the three wrapped the remaining bread
in a newspaper.

"Take this with you, Alexandra Lvovna," he said.

"Thank you, Vania!"

I hurried away, stumbling in the dark without my glasses,
with my painted face, and my loaf of bread under my arm.
The joy of seeing my sister, the kindness of the three peasants,
and Vania's smile meant more to me than the hope of freedom.

XXXV

NICHOLAS AND ANNIE

OUR cell was frigid; we received hardly any wood for heating. I caught cold and went to the dispensary to get some aspirin. In the corridor the nurse stopped me.

"Your name is Tolstoy?"

"Yes."

"Were you kept in the prison of the Secret Police?"

"Yes. But it doesn't concern you, does it?" I said tartly.

We all knew that spies were set to watch the political prisoners in the camp, so we tried to avoid speaking to people we did not know.

"Have you forgotten the officer's wife?"

"The officer's wife? Do you know her? Where is she? How can I find her?"

"She was shot."

"Shot?"

"Yes."

"And Nicholas? Where is he? Is he alive?"

"Yes, he lives with his sister."

"Do you know his address? For mercy's sake, give it to me."

"They live in the same place, on the other side of the Moscow River."

She tore off a scrap of paper and wrote the address.

I had a fever that night. The cell seemed suffocatingly hot. I slept little and was tormented by dreams.

I saw the fat woman shot. Her stout body became stiff and shapeless. Soldiers with pointed helmets turned it over, searching for diamonds. Her face was dreadful. Her puffy cheeks had hardened; her small round mouth was open and disfigured, and the blue eyes were glassy. As the soldiers turned her body, her plump white hand scraped on the stone floor. The sound filled the cell.

I could bear it no longer. I got up and flung off my blankets. All my body was on fire. I lay down again and tried not to think of her, but my thoughts returned to her again and again.

"How could they do that? A human being like myself—a withered, flabby, gray-haired woman shot in the back."

"It's impossible," I exclaimed.

My neighbor awoke.

"What did you say? What is the matter with you?"

"I have a fever. Will you get me some water?" She got up and brought me a big mug of cold water. For a few minutes I felt better. But I knew she would lie down and fall asleep, and I should again be left alone with my dreadful thoughts. As soon as I shut my eyes I saw the same scene. Toward dawn, quite exhausted, I fell asleep. I woke up with the feeling that something terrible had happened. "The officer's wife has been shot." And I knew that I should never forget it.

SEVERAL months later I was freed. At home once more, I thought of the diamonds. The clay pot was still standing on the shelf in the kitchen. I wrote to Nicholas and Annie, and they came—a girl of twenty and a tall bony lad of seventeen. Annie was poorly dressed, but her clothes were neat and clean. Nicholas was haggard, dirty, and very pale. He either did not know how or did not want to hide his misery. His trousers were in tatters, his shoes split, and while we talked he kept trying to draw down his sleeves which were too short.

"Are you Nicholas and Annie?"

"Yes."

"Have you any papers to prove it?"

I asked the stupid formal question, afraid to show my emotion.

Annie opened her shabby old handbag.

I did not even glance at the papers, but hurried to the kitchen, blew the dust off the flowerpot, and emptied out the earth around the dead plant. The oilcloth was dry and stuck together. I unwrapped it.

"Here, Nicholas, your mother gave me these for you."

"Mother?"

"Yes, I could not get them to you before. Your address was taken away from me by the Secret Police."

"Mother? How? When did you . . . ?"

"In the prison of the Secret Police. You were on the floor above us. Don't you remember? You sent your mother sugar and herrings."

"Mother! Mother!" he gasped. "You know they have . . ."

He covered his face with his hands.

In a few days they came again to ask me where they could sell some of the jewels.

"We are so badly off," Annie said. "Nicholas must go to school. He must buy clothes, books and, oh, we have not had enough to eat for such a long time!"

She seemed to be excusing herself.

"Of course you must sell them."

"But we are afraid. We don't know where to go. They say people are put in prison for selling jewels now."

I gave them the address of a man I could trust. They seemed to be more happy and calm when they left me. I never saw them again.

XXXVI

KALININ

W ELL, here you are! Free and ready to start counter-revolutionary work again?"

"You are mistaken, Michael Ivanovich! I hate your politics and will have nothing to do with them!"

Kalinin looked at me searchingly.

"Tell me, how did you find our prisons? More like convalescent homes?"

"No, Michael Ivanovich."

"You are spoiled—accustomed to luxury. But imagine what it's like for a workman, a real proletarian!"

"It is hideous! The prisoners are starving, the buildings are filthy, cold in winter . . ."

"But, as I understand, you yourself have been doing educational work, organizing schools and lectures. There was nothing of the kind in the old prisons. Our government is concerned with making the prisoners conscientious, literate citizens."

I tried to argue, to tell the "Elder of All Russia," as Kalinin is called, about the conditions in prison, but it was useless.

"You are prejudiced, Alexandra Lvovna! Of course, there may be defects, but, as a whole, our prisons are good and cannot be compared with any other prisons in the world!"

My objections were disagreeable to Kalinin.

"Just like the old *régime*," I thought to myself, "deceiving himself and others."

It seemed strange that this half-literate man who had belonged to the working class, who was neither stupid nor ill intentioned, had so soon lost touch with his own people, without even realizing it. He no longer felt their misery, their oppression and misfortunes.

"Everything is exaggerated," he said. "They keep saying that people are starving, that there is no food. I wanted to find out the truth for myself. I went to a restaurant, right here on the Mokhovaya. Incognito, of course. Do you know what they served me? Caviar, sturgeon, and wonderful pies. . . . And it was not expensive!"

I laughed.

"Do you seriously think, Michael Ivanovich, that you were not recognized? Your portraits are hanging everywhere."

"I don't think that I was," he said. "Now what food do you have. What did you have for dinner today?"

"Potatoes, fried with castor oil."

"Hm . . . What else?"

"Nothing else today. Sometimes I have cabbage soup, without meat of course, millet cereal . . ."

"That's not so good! Well, what can I do for you?"

ONCE Kalinin was especially cordial. I was in the reception room, talking to his secretary—a stylishly dressed, dark, handsome young woman with a magnificent coiffure, polished nails and fine manners—when he saw me.

"Come in, come in!" he called, "I have representatives from Siberia, grand people!"

His visitors were three peasants and they were certainly splendid: big fellows with long beards, peasant fur coats and felt boots. There was a calm dignity about them very different from Kalinin's nervousness and fussiness. In a businesslike manner they stated their case: A Soviet farm had taken meadows belonging to their village. It was a common story. Local Communists, intoxicated by their unaccustomed power, interpreted the laws in their own way and "curved the line," as they used to say in Moscow. Kalinin listened, nodding his head, and asked questions, trying to talk as the peasants did.

Of course there were a great many such complaints against the local Communists, and Kalinin had no time to hear them all; but sometimes when the offended party succeeded in seeing him, the "line" was straightened.

Usually the "Elder of All Russia" received the petitioners in the general reception room. There was always a crowd of them. Kalinin went from one to another, trying to get each story as quickly as possible and hurrying on to the next, while his secretary followed, writing down the petitions and the decisions. Then, in the same hurried way, he walked out, and the crowd continued sometimes for hours to await his next entrance.

"If your father were alive, how happy he would be to see what we have done for the working classes," Kalinin said to me once.

"I do not think so!"

"What do you mean? Didn't he himself struggle against the old government for the welfare of the masses?"

"Oh, yes, but terror, exile, capital punishment, no freedom— all that would have been unbearable to him!"

"Oh, those are only temporary measures. But how about land for the working class? the eight-hour day? And . . ."

"Shall I tell you the truth?" I interrupted. "If my father were alive, he would have written another *I Cannot Be Silent*. And who knows, perhaps you would have put him in prison for counterrevolution!"

The handsome secretary came in several times and reminded the "Elder" about business and the crowd of petitioners waiting for him, but he paid no attention. He was excited, paced the room, smoked nervously, and argued with me for more than an hour.

Kalinin had visited Yasnaia Poliana while I was in prison. My sister had shown him father's home, told him about father's ideas, and described his fight against the old government and against capital punishment.

"Oh! Tatiana Lvovna," Kalinin had said, in a low voice, "you know, I have to sign death sentences sometimes . . ."

In 1922 I pleaded with Kalinin in behalf of seven old clergymen who had been sentenced to death. The government had ordered church treasure confiscated, and the measure was not accepted passively everywhere. In some places the population met the soldiers and the Komsomols with stones. The government replied with a reign of terror. Clergymen suffered most of all. Many of the best of them were shot.

One of my friends, imprisoned with the seven clergymen who were condemned to death, told me about their last days. Knowing that no one would bury them with Orthodox rites, and suffering from the thought of having no religious ceremony, they received extreme unction from each other, and performed the burial service over one another.

I do not remember what I said to Kalinin, I only know that I spoke fervently, and he, as he always did when excited, smoked and strode up and down the room. All at once he stopped.

"Why are you tormenting me like this?" he exclaimed. "I can't do anything! How do you know? Perhaps I was the only one in the Central Executive Committee who was against their execution. *I cannot do anything!*"

XXXVII

YASNAIA POLIANA

I DO not remember when it first occurred to me to start educational work at Yasnaia Poliana. The first incentive may have been the poor administration of Prince Obolensky and the "benefactor," who took no interest in the estate or in the welfare of the peasants. It is true that they made "gifts" to the peasants but these gifts had a somewhat demoralizing influence, making the people think that without the slightest effort on their part they had a right to certain privileges.

On the other hand, imprisonment and lack of work that I cared for had had their effect on me. I thought a great deal about Yasnaia Poliana. I imagined the district provided with schools, hospitals, libraries and coöperatives; I pictured the peasants improving their farms and way of living, their children getting an education and all the advantages of the city without having to break away from the country. And I was concerned, too, about my father's house. It seemed to me that the only way the estate could be made really safe was to have the house made into a museum and the rest of the estate attached to it as a kind of memorial.

With these ideas I went to Kalinin. He listened to me attentively.

"All right, give me your proposal, I'll support it!"

For several weeks Sergius Sukhotin[1] and I worked on the project, pondering over each word, trying to bring in father's ideas and at the same time make it acceptable to the government.

At last it was ready. On the tenth of June, 1921, I was summoned to a meeting of the Praesidium of the Central Executive Committee.

It was a bright, sunny morning. I bicycled to the Kremlin,

[1] My sister Tania's stepson, who took part in the murder of Rasputin with Prince Yusupov. He married Sophie Tolstoy, the daughter of my brother Andrew.

taking side streets and avoiding traffic. At the gate a soldier stopped me.

"Where are you going, comrade?"

"To the meeting of the Praesidium."

"Show me your papers!"

He took my pass and telephoned to the secretary. Permission was given for me to enter.

Leaving my bicycle near the gate, I hurried uphill, past the "Tsar Cannon" and the "Tsar Bell,"[2] and turned right into what had been the Court of Justice in prerevolutionary days. Again a soldier stopped me and I showed my pass. Here, in a small room, at a table covered with a red cloth, the meeting was being held. I took a chair by the wall and waited, nervously running over all the arguments I could use if the scheme met with opposition.

At last my turn came. The secretary explained the plan briefly. Three or four questions were asked. Someone suggested changing the word "commissar" to "curator" in paragraph three.

"Yes, that will fit the Tolstoy organization better," Kalinin said.

The project was adopted. All my worry was needless. A wide field of interesting and responsible work opened before me.

DECREE

OF THE CENTRAL EXECUTIVE COMMITTEE CONCERNING YASNAIA POLIANA

1. The estate of Yasnaia Poliana situated in the Krapivna district of Tula Province with the house, furniture, park, orchard, forests and woods, fields and meadows, waste land and out-buildings, is the national property of the RSFSR.

2. The management and the administration of the whole shall be under the control of the Department of Museum Activities in the Commissariat of Education, which cares for all monuments, works of art, and antiquities.

3. In accordance with Section 2, the Commissariat of Education,

---

[2] Relics of old Muscovite Russia, both dating originally from the end of the sixteenth century. The bell, which weighs two thousand tons, was recast in 1735.

with the approval of the Tula Provincial Executive Committee, shall appoint a curator. In case of any dispute, the final decision shall lie in the hands of the All-Russian Central Executive Committee.

4. The curator shall care for the House-Museum, with all the furniture; the grave of L. N. Tolstoy, with the forests and woods surrounding it, the park, the gardens, and all the out-buildings, preserving the place in its original state, restoring anything that has deteriorated or been destroyed since the death of Tolstoy.

5. The curator shall establish at Yasnaia Poliana an educational center, with a library and reading room and schools, and shall organize readings and lectures of the widest educational character, especially concerning Tolstoy; plays, scientific exhibits, excursions, and so on.

6. In case it should be found necessary to build new houses, and impossible to adapt the old ones to the purposes enumerated in Section 5, the curator shall report to the Commissariat of Education, and it shall be his duty to see that the new buildings do not change the general aspect of the historical estate.

7. The curator shall determine the number of employees required for the work mentioned in Sections 4, 5 and 6, and shall report it to the Museum Department for approval in the usual way.

8. The employees shall be selected by the curator and approved by the Museum Department.

9. The fields, vegetable gardens and meadows, as well as the orchard that belongs to the estate, shall be cultivated by a community of Tolstoy's disciples under the auspices of the Commissariat of Agriculture, in such a way that the farm by its methods shall approach the model type of experimental farm and shall be an example to the surrounding population and visitors to Yasnaia Poliana.

10. The charter of the Commune, as well as its members and the changes that may take place in them, shall be approved by the Commissariat of Agriculture, with the consent of the curator of Yasnaia Poliana and the representative of the community.

11. The curator of Yasnaia Poliana has the right to impose a veto on any decision of the community that may not accord with work of an historical or educational character.

12. The forests and woods shall be cared for by the Tolstoyan community under the supervision of the curator of Yasnaia Poliana.

13. The community shall have the right, free of charge, to use for

its work such live stock, movables and immovables as the curator shall find possible to lend or provide, without harming the buildings which have historical value.

14. The curator of Yasnaia Poliana shall have the right to communicate with central and local government establishments concerning matters touching Yasnaia Poliana, and also with private establishments authorized by the government.

15. Every citizen of the RSFSR shall have free admission to Yasnaia Poliana at hours and on days to be fixed by the curator.

16. The curator, together with the representative of the community, may allow the closest relatives of Tolstoy to live in Yasnaia Poliana and may allow those who were friends of Tolstoy to visit and stay in Yasnaia Poliana with free lodging for a time to be fixed by the curator and the representative of the community.

17. In order to make it easier for all citizens and especially students who want to visit Yasnaia Poliana and the historical estate, with the approval of the Commissariat of Transportation, at least once a week a special car shall be attached to one of the passenger trains running between Moscow and Yasnaia Poliana.

18. This decree shall be in effect upon being signed, and may be changed and broadened according to future decisions of the Central Executive Committee on the recommendation of the Commissariat of Education.

President KALININ, *Secretary* ENUKIDZE.

XXXVIII

MITROFAN

MITROFAN came in the spring of 1921 as the representative of the Tolstoyan agricultural community. I do not remember where he came from or who recommended him. He was said to be stubborn and strong willed but a good organizer. I welcomed his coming: he was to relieve me of the responsibility for organizing the Tolstoyan community and running the farm, and leave me free to devote myself to the schools and museums. He was a tall dark-bearded person with a high voice and a peculiar giggle which did not seem appropriate to his size. I grew to dislike him, although I tried to persuade myself that there was no reason for it.

There were other things to worry about. On the twenty-third of April, 1921, Lenin's famous New Economic Policy was announced. Private trade was to be allowed, and employees were to receive wages and buy things for themselves. The government would no longer supply the population with food. The time of reorganization was hard. Wages were very low—for teachers, three to seven rubles a month. As yet there was no food to be bought on the market. The inhabitants of Yasnaia Poliana were worried. "As soon as Alexandra Lvovna takes over the administration of Yasnaia Poliana," they said, "our food cards are taken away." Most of them were indignant— either secretly or openly. They remembered the "father-benefactor," who got them everything they needed, up to candy and toilet soap; and they were sorry for Prince Obolensky, who would have to leave with his family and look for other work. Everyone was dissatisfied with the new order. Many lost their jobs; the peasants were deprived of lands belonging to the estate which they had cultivated for half the crops. I had a difficult time trying to combat the dissatisfaction and the antagonistic attitude toward the Tolstoyans and myself, and start my work.

I made another trip to Moscow. When I came back, all the crops were gone from the fields, and the barn was empty. Obolensky and his helpers had hurriedly harvested everything while I was away and disposed of it. I was left with an estate full of people and animals, and no food for them. I was wild with indignation and anxiety. What could I do? Quarrel with Obolensky's people? That would help my feelings very little as many of them were my relatives, and it would have no effect on the food supply. I urged Mitrofan to organize the Tolstoyan community as quickly as possible. The sooner we had our own organization started and got rid of all the old employees of Obolensky the better. But Mitrofan did nothing about it.

Obolensky's helpers were belligerent and so terrified the Tolstoyans that they were afraid to go out at night. Mitrofan assured me that the young people who were devoted to Obolensky had threatened to kill him, and begged me to defend him. I paid no attention. It seemed to me that a strong man with several young friends could protect himself from danger, and I did not believe there was any. He insisted that once when he went into the orchard to get some apples someone shot at him.

One morning when I got up, I was told that Mitrofan had disappeared. He could not be found on the estate nor in the village. He simply vanished.

XXXIX

SALT AND STURGEON

COMRADE KHALATOV was the head of the Commissariat of Food Supplies. The sight of him reminded me of how my little brother Vanichka used to ask: "Mother, is that a man, or is it in fun?" But Comrade Khalatov was not "in fun"—for all his great black eyes, regular features, long hair floating about his shoulders, his velvet blouse and Armenian fez. He was a commissar, and the life of the Russian people greatly depended on him.

"Do you know," he said, "that following Lenin's decree all the government establishments must provide for themselves and the Commissariat of Food Supplies will be liquidated? But we have some food left and we'll share it with you."

He took a pencil: "Flour, sugar, cereal—do you want American beans?"

"Please, could you give us salt?"

"We have no salt. What else? Sturgeon?"

"Sturgeon?"

He smiled. "Why, yes. Does that astonish you? Don't you want sturgeon?"

"Thank you. It seems such a luxury."

I was delighted. Now I had to get a freight car to ship all these goods to Yasnaia Poliana, and I went to Kalinin. The words, "went to Khalatov," "went to Kalinin," sound simple enough, but it was not an easy task to get to them. Sometimes one had to wait for weeks, sometimes for months for a pass. But this time everything favored me. Kalinin received me at once and gave me a note to the Commissariat of Transportation. He also gave me salt. It happened that he had just been south and had brought a carload back with him.

"Is eight hundred pounds enough?"

It was good salt and lasted us for years under the name of "Kalinin's salt."

Sergius Sukhotin and a young girl who was going to Yasnaia and I rode with the freight the one hundred and thirty miles. For two days our train stood ten miles outside Moscow and no one understood why. It was very hot. On the third day, Sergius and I rolled up our sleeves and began rubbing the inside of the huge sturgeons with salt. We worked half a day, and our hands were covered with blisters. We washed in ponds and rivers near the stations where the train stopped, slept for seven nights on bags of American beans, and on the eighth day reached Yasnaia Poliana, very tired and dirty but content. Nothing could enhance our authority in the eyes of the people on the estate as much as this load of food.

"Now, didn't I tell you?" auntie said. "She got it, didn't she? And sturgeon. You didn't even dream of sturgeon in the time of the 'benefactor.'"

Now that everyone was satisfied, I could at last turn my attention to the schools and the museum.

XL

STARTING THE SCHOOL

THERE had been no good school in Yasnaia since my father gave up teaching. In the days before the Revolution, I sent a petition to the head of our zemstvo in the Krapivna district, asking him to open a zemstvo school in our village, but his answer was that the church parish school had to remain there *forever,* and that there could be no other in Yasnaia Poliana.

And so this old two-class school was the only one, and continued to be after the Revolution; but now it was a Soviet school, and belonged to the district Department of People's Education. The same teachers were there—two daughters of the village priest—and I am sure that their methods of teaching never changed.

Besides this school building, we had at our disposal for the first year an old abandoned kitchen. The beams were rotten, and some of the ends hung from the ceiling. The teacher and his students propped them up so that the place could be used safely. In the morning, the boys learned carpentering; in the afternoon, one of the Tolstoyans taught them reading and writing and arithmetic. There were no teaching schedules then, and no textbooks. The Commissariat of Education had just been organized, and no one yet understood its functions. Old methods were abandoned, but no sooner were new methods adopted than they were changed to newer ones.

The sabotage on the part of the intelligentsia that characterized the first years of the Revolution was over. The intellectuals came back to work; many experienced teachers assisted the Commissariat of Education in trying to bring some system and order into the schools. Many of us believed that we could not only save the old treasures of Russian culture, but could build up new ones, and these hopes filled our lives.

To my great astonishment and disappointment, I got no sympathy for my work from the Tolstoyans. They declared bluntly that they despised education and culture, "just like Tolstoy," and they ridiculed all my plans. When I asked them to help with the educational work, they refused. They would not give us horses for the school workers or for bringing books from the city for our village library. At the same time, they had a hard time getting along. To help them out, I invited several young men to work in the schools and museum for wages and food.

The inhabitants of Yasnaia Poliana disliked the Tolstoyans, and hated one Gushchin especially. He was a dirty, illiterate young fellow with uncombed hair, filthy clothes and great self-assurance. All day long he would strut about the yard, giving advice or orders to his companions, or he would harness my favorite stallion, Osman, and drive off, bringing the handsome horse back in a lather.

"The idea of bringing all those loafers to Yasnaia Poliana!" grumbled the cook, one-eyed Nikolayevna, when I went into the kitchen. "What did we need them for, the do-nothings, the God-forgive-me trash!"

"Stop it, Nikolayevna!" I interrupted sharply, feeling in the depths of my heart that the old woman was right. "They are good idealistic people, they help everybody. . . . You should be ashamed to talk that way! They drive you to the city when you want to go. Who took you to Tula yesterday—Gushchin?"

"Gushchin, Gushchin, *nie tuda pushchen!*[1] He goes right into Tatiana Lvovna's room without even knocking, and sits down in an easy chair in front of her! A muzhik! 'Idealistic!' Oh, God!"

Instead of Mitrofan, Bulgakov, the brother of father's secretary, was elected representative. He was a young student who knew nothing about farming, and was afraid to contradict the Tolstoyans on questions of educational and museum work.

"I wanted to tell you, Sasha," auntie said, "I think you did

[1] Gushchin, Gushchin
Went where he shouldn't have been.

well to send the 'benefactor' and the others away. . . . But you were wrong to let those tramps in, and you will see that for yourself. They are lazy and impudent. Yesterday I passed the Remington room[2] and saw someone lying on the couch. I went back to look twice, and raised my lorgnette. It was—oh! what's his name?—you know, he talked about Beethoven . . ."

"I don't know, Auntie."

"Of course you know—a big, good-looking fellow—he asked Lenochka to teach him French . . ."

"Valerian?"

"Yes, yes, Valerian! 'Are you sick, Valerian?' I asked, and kept on looking at him through the lorgnette. And he answered as calmly as possible: 'No, Tatiana Andreyevna, thank you, I am quite well, but I am me-di-ta-ting!' And he continued lying there with his arms under his head. Well, I got angry and told him that if he wanted to visit a decent house, he had no right to lie on sofas! Just think of it: with an old lady standing and speaking to him, he lies there and meditates!"

The Tolstoyans did not know how to work. They had no discipline or system, they did everything carelessly. When they went to get water, they overturned the barrel. When they hauled manure to the fields, their carts stuck somewhere in the mud or snow. The peasants watched them and shook their heads.

"Volodia!" they would shout to a long, bony, red-haired fellow, "don't you see that your horse is unharnessed?"

I lost patience, and began to wonder what was the use of having all those people on the estate who did not help with the educational work, and could not even do their own jobs.

The "brothers" left. Only a few of them stayed as employees of the museum and the schools. After their departure a picture was found on the wall of the dormitory. It was a caricature of me, blowing soap bubbles. The bubbles—labeled museum, schools, hospital, library—flew in different directions and burst.

Later on, Gushchin and other Tolstoyans became Bolsheviks. I met Gushchin several times in the Tula Executive Commit-

[2] So named for the typewriter we used there.

tee. His hair was combed and greased, his suit was new and his shoes shiny. His attitude toward me was condescending and patronizing. He was press correspondent of the Tula Executive Committee.

The red-haired Volodia also became a Communist.

Instead of a Tolstoyan community, we organized an agricultural coöperative for all the employees of Yasnaia Poliana.

XLI

FARMING

IT is as warm as summer. The horse is slowly dragging the sled through the last snow which is well mixed with dirt. Around the hot beds, the snow has melted and on the bare patches dark green nettles are already growing. Skylarks are singing in the fields. I turn the horse and back him, holding the reins in my right hand and dumping over the sled of warm steaming manure with my left. Osman, my favorite brown stallion, is not as obedient as the other horses. He is impatient, beats the ground with his hooves, neighs, and as soon as he feels the load off, plays and pulls on the reins.

"Whoa! Easy there."

I am afraid that I shall not work as well as the others, so I try to take the largest pieces of manure on my fork and load my sled quickly. The work is not hard, but the others make it uncomfortable for me.

"You must not tire yourself too much, Your Excellency," the overseer, Adrian Pavlovich, says. "You had better go and rest while we finish this."

"You old . . . you'll get us both in prison! Do you understand?" I shout to him. "No 'Excellency!' If the Bolsheviks hear it, what will happen?"

"Excuse me, Your . . . Alexandra Lvovna! I can't possibly get used to it!"

"Vasili Vasilievich!" the peasant girls call to the bookkeeper. "The wheelbarrow is too heavy for you. Don't strain your belly!"

His white well-kept hands, accustomed to do nothing more than write figures, tremble, but the bookkeeper is trying to be cheerful and smiles.

Father's old valet, Ilya Vasilievich, is also working.

"Go away, go and lie down on the stove!" the girls shout. "We'll get along without you."

"Yes, Ilya Vasilievich," Adrian Pavlovich says, "you'd better go."

But the old man, thin and feeble, continues working, paying no attention to anybody.

We were glad to be working, but also, like all the members of the coöperative, we knew that farming was our only salvation from hunger, and we worked with triple energy. Everything went well during the summer of 1922, and one task followed another. From the vegetable garden, we moved into the fields and planted potatoes and beets. We had plenty of milk, the cows were well cared for, and the dairy in good order.

There was plenty to do. Every little while, I had to run into the office, give the necessary orders, sign papers, or show tourists around the museum. The rest of the time I was farming.

Hay was plentiful. The rye, too, was excellent; but when the mowing machine cut it, it got tangled. Even the experienced workers had difficulty in binding it up.

I was so tired after the first morning's work in the rye fields that I could hardly get home. After lunch it was easier, but the next day all my body ached. I could hardly move. On the third day, I worked like the others.

Loading the sheaves on the carts was as easy as playing tennis. You speared a sheaf with a fork and tossed it up to someone on the load who caught it in his hands. Then you tied up the load and sat down on the sheaves to wait for the next cart. The field was clear and shone like gold; only here and there cornflowers and wormwood could be seen. The straw heated by the sun smelled like fresh-baked black bread. From far off came the sound of the empty carts hurrying back to the fields. I felt very warm, strong, and happy.

Once some peasants came to the field. They had no business with us at all. They were only curious to see our farming. They stood and looked.

"Our rye's not as good," they said.

I was proud. It was the greatest compliment we could have been paid.

Sometimes, when the work was very hard or it was hot, we

had tea in the fields, taking sugar and tea from our scanty store of provisions. We sat under a shock of grain, and two pails of hot water were brought. My companions bit off pieces of sugar and sucked their tea through them to make it last longer. They drank and perspired and wiped their foreheads with their aprons and handkerchiefs, until the two pails were empty. Then they stood up with shining faces.

"How much stronger we are now," Adrian Pavlovich would say. "Now we can go on without resting till evening!"

When autumn came and we divided our crops, we found that we had so much that we could even sell some of the vegetables. There was plenty of bread and cereal, too. Everybody was happy.

"The Bolsheviks keep on talking about the eight-hour day," Adrian Pavlovich said. "Stupid! How could we have got so much if we had worked only eight hours? But now, thank God, we have everything, and people are envious of us."

XLII

HOW WE HELPED THE FAMISHED

THERE was a terrible famine in the provinces on the Volga, in Crimea, and other parts of Russia between 1920 and 1922. It was more talked of in Moscow than anything else, but the wretched condition of all Russians at that time—lacking food, clothes, and money—prevented them from taking relief measures. Everybody else was half-starved, too. My nephew Ilya and some of his friends were happy to be able to work with the American Relief Association and some Quaker organizations. Peasants in the regions where straw was used for fuel were burning chunks of their thatched roofs. Samples of bread with clay in it were passed around Moscow.

One day in 1921 a friend telephoned me and said:

"We are organizing a committee to help the famished. Will you consent to be on it?"

"Yes, of course I want to help the famished. But how?"

"Oh, everything is settled with the government. We thought of giving you a mission to Canada. You may be able to get bread from the Dukhobors for their starving brothers on the Volga."

The new committee was not exactly a private affair. At the head of it was the President of the Moscow Soviet—Comrade Kamenev.[1]

At this time the intelligentsia in Moscow were beginning to say: We must do something! We must apply our knowledge and experience to the welfare of the masses. Some went even further and admitted: If we had not opposed the government in the early days of the Revolution, Russia would not be suffering now from famine and the breakdown of industry of all kinds. It was hopeless to look for rescue from the White gen-

---

[1] During the dictatorship of Stalin, Kamenev was said to be in the opposition. He was dismissed, exiled, and later on was given some unimportant position.

erals, the Denikins and Kolchaks. We must collaborate with
the Bolsheviks, we must try to influence them for good, and
help them. And then little by little they will become more reasonable. This is the only way to progress. Things can't go on
long as they are now.

Many well-educated men once more felt firm ground under
their feet. They were no longer without place or use, they were
human beings who were called on to help other human beings.

Not all of my friends joined the society. Some were skeptical. They smiled significantly, and not only refused to work
with us, but advised us to give up the "adventure," as they
called it. I paid no attention to their warnings. The temptation
was too great. I had been imprisoned for counterrevolution,
and now I had a chance to do work for the people.

When I arrived at the place of meeting there were sixty or
seventy men and women there—talking in small groups, discussing ways and means of organizing. They were all well-
known people: professors, doctors, lawyers, economists, scientists—the best of Moscow society. Among them was the small
youthful-seeming Vera Nikolayevna Figner, the famous revolutionary, who had been kept in prison under the Tsar for
about twenty years because of her work for the freedom of
Russia. Her hair had only a few silver threads, her eyes were
young and bright. She wore a plain black dress with snow-
white collar and cuffs.

We were waiting for our president, Comrade Kamenev. We
waited a quarter of an hour, half an hour, an hour—patiently.
Kamenev alone had the authority to set us to work. Only two
or three began grumbling.

"Don't you think it's a crime to make us wait so long?"
somebody whispered.

"It's not very noble to take advantage of one's position like
that."

"Noble? it's beastly!" exclaimed a zemstvo doctor, who was
well known because he had been imprisoned a great many
times—under the Tsar for his liberal ideas, and during the

Revolution as a counterrevolutionist. "If it were not for the aim of our assembly, I should have gone home immediately!"

"The president gives himself airs."

"Here he is!" somebody exclaimed, and at that moment, under the windows of the old-fashioned two-story house we heard the roar of motor cars.

The doors were flung open and a dozen soldiers in the uniform of the Secret Police, with peaked helmets, revolvers and rifles, burst into the hall.

"Citizens! You are arrested!"

"What? . . . Why? Where is Comrade Kamenev? We must see him!" people cried. "There is certainly some misunderstanding! We will wait for Kamenev!"

"Whew!" whistled the officer. "You'll wait a long time! Come on. We've no time to waste."

"But Comrade Kamenev knows all about the committee," we protested. "He is the president of it."

The excitement was so great, and the people who surrounded the chief were so exasperated, that even the Chekist was confused.

"Well," he said, "it isn't my fault. I get an order and have to obey. If Kamenev didn't want you to be arrested, he could have stopped it, I guess. He's not coming. And now, move. I have orders to take all of you to the Cheka. Do you understand?"

We understood perfectly. All at once there was absolute silence in the hall.

"Comrade Figner!" roared the chief.

"Well, what do you want?" asked the revolutionary, stepping out of the crowd. "What do you want of me?"

"You are free and can go home."

The blood rushed to the old lady's face.

"Why should *I* go home?" she asked.

"I have a special order not to arrest you. You are free."

"But I do not want to be free!" she exclaimed, and her voice trembled with excitement. "I am as guilty as all these friends of mine. I am also on the committee."

"That doesn't concern me," the soldier said as he turned

away. Vera Figner was left alone while the rest of us were led out of the hall and loaded into the cars.

Some of us were let out of prison in a few days, some in a few months; but not one of us ever received an explanation of our arrest from Comrade Kamenev or from the government.

XLIII

COW BARNS AND CLASSROOMS

I THOUGHT we were going to see the school . . ."

"Yes, don't be afraid, the bull is tied. Will you come in?"

We walked over straw mixed with cow dung, past the ruminating cows which watched us with large indifferent eyes. A great dark-headed Swiss bull turned to look at us as we passed.

"But isn't this a cow barn?"

"Yes and no . . . it's not exactly a cow barn. Now please, the school is to the left."

We entered a large light room with wide windows on both sides, new wooden floors, and whitewashed walls.[1] There were twelve benches in the room and twenty boys were busy carpentering.

"A month ago this was a cow shed, too," I said. "The other side, where you saw the cows, we expect to make into lodgings for the teachers."

The old professor, an inspector for the Commissariat of Education, shook his fluffy white mane and smiled, showing a single yellow protruding tusk.

The instructor met us—a carpenter, a big fair-haired man in a Russian shirt and high boots, with a jolly, laughing face. He loved his work and his students. He was eager to tell the inspector about his plans for the future organization of the workshops. He and his boys, with the simplest carpenter's tools, had just finished fixing over the room.

We continued to lack school buildings. In 1922 I had an estimate made on a school to be built in memory of my father, and presented it to the Commissariat of Education. The govern-

[1] This building was built between one hundred seventy and two hundred years ago by my father's grandfather, Prince Volkonsky, and was used for spinning and weaving in the times of serfdom. Later on most of it was made over into a stable. The building was not repaired and fell into decay, but was rebuilt in 1928 for Tolstoy's jubilee. It was said to have been constructed by a famous Italian architect.

ment had no money and the project was delayed; meanwhile
new children wanted to come to school and we could only admit a small percentage of them. We rented a simple hut in the
village and taught two sessions.

Our organization grew rapidly. As soon as we opened a
school it was full of pupils. I was kept busy making trips to
Moscow for textbooks and school equipment.

Once an official in the Commissariat of Education asked me
what my position in the Yasnaia Poliana schools was.

"Why, I don't know," I answered. "I am curator of Yasnaia
Poliana."

"Yes, you are under the Museum Department as curator of
the museum; but you are organizing schools, and you have to
deal with the Department of Education in your school work."

It was true, although I had never thought about it.

"Do you get wages?"

"No."

"How do you live?"

"I sell honey."

The official laughed. He might not have laughed if he had
known how hard it was to carry those heavy linden casks on
my shoulders every time I went to Moscow. Selling honey was
my only income. The Bolsheviks had nationalized all the Tolstoy property except the bees.

"All right. We will appoint you the director of the Yasnaia
Poliana school and give you wages."

So it was arranged that I was to be paid forty-two rubles and
fifty kopeks a month.

In the autumn of 1923 the Jewish American organization,
"Agrojoint," through their representative, Mr. Rosen, gave us
ten thousand rubles, and with this we put up a building that
was used for the first four classes of the high school.[2] The oldest children still had to be taught in the village hut. At the same
time, we received some money from the government for the

2 There are seven grades in the usual Russian high school and four in the primary school. By 1929 we had at Yasnaia Poliana four primary schools and three high
schools. The high schools were a seven-year industrial school, a nine-year agricultural school, and the memorial school which also had nine grades.

memorial school. We did not want to change the appearance of the estate, so we asked the peasants to give us a few acres of land for the school. Several meetings were held while I was in Moscow. My assistants talked to the peasants about the necessity for a school and the benefit of instruction for their children, but to no avail. The peasants simply refused.

"You do not teach religion in your schools. Why do we need them?" they said.

I called one more meeting when I got back from the city, and the peasants grudgingly consented to give us about three acres for the new school, but I felt that they gave it, not because they wanted the school, but because they did not want to displease me.

One enterprise led to another. The appearance of some ten orphans from I don't know where, who had to be taken care of, led to the opening of an orphan home. Also the American Relief Association presented us with medical supplies and a set of instruments, so we opened a dispensary.

It was a difficult task to get money for all these activities. I had to spend long hours waiting in the reception rooms of commissars, explaining, arguing. Sometimes the central authorities turned the matter over to the local authorities. Then I knew that my case was lost. The local Soviets had very little money, and would not bother with Yasnaia Poliana.

After the dispensary was opened in a small house in the village, we realized how the population needed it. Later on, we organized a clinic for mothers and children, and several nurseries; and in 1928, the hundredth anniversary of my father's birth, a hospital was built.

By 1924 our small, poorly equipped school bore the name of "The Educational Experiment Station of Yasnaia Poliana," although hardly any experimental work was done. "We are giving you your title in advance," the Commissariat of Education told us.

Salaries were so low and conditions so hard that we had trouble finding teachers for our schools. We had no lodgings. A great number of our teachers had to live in peasant huts in

the village. For more than a year, we could not find a teacher
of physics and chemistry. At last we got a woman from Siberia.
Although she had been told that life at Yasnaia Poliana was
rough, she never expected to find it so bad. Living too close to
the calves, cattle, and sheep, she was miserable, wept during
most of the winter, and in the spring returned to Siberia.

The courses of study in the high schools worked out quite
spontaneously. The nine-year school emphasized agricultural
subjects, the seven-year school industrial ones.

We needed agricultural work. Farming was at a low level in
our district. The three-field system of crop rotation was practiced in the old-fashioned way. The cows were few, poorly
cared for, and gave little milk. The peasants could not make a
living by farming, and had to work in town as cab drivers. Our
nine-year school set out to teach agriculture to the students and
help the peasants in their work. The farm belonging to the museum of Yasnaia Poliana was to be a model, where experimental work could be done. In 1924 the agricultural coöperative
was abandoned, as the museum workers were too busy to farm,
and the museum farm took its place. This was worked by hired
hands and run for profit, to support the museum.

The industrial school trained locksmiths and carpenters so
that they could mend machinery and make furniture in the
winter months when outside work was impossible. Yasnaia
Poliana is surrounded by forests and much of the timber is excellent for carpentering. We had ambitious plans, but their re-
alization was difficult. The industrial school was closed several
times, because the government would not give money for keeping it up; and again and again it was transferred from one department to another. We did not want to abandon the school
because we felt that it was needed. It was always full of pupils.
The peasants realized that here they could learn a trade which
would enable them to earn a living; and the boys liked the
work. In the daytime they studied; in the evening they returned to the workshops and made furniture—tables, chairs,
chests, and trunks for their families.

The cow barn that we had made over into workshops was

too small. We were flooded with applications for entrance to
the industrial school, and there were hundreds of boys that we
could not admit. I could not bear the sight of little chaps coming on foot for miles, and begging to be admitted. They would
stand watching the boys who had been admitted, and sometimes cry bitterly if we refused to let them in.

The houses in the village were full of students. They came
from distant villages, went home each weekend and brought
their food back with them. Sometimes they paid a ruble or two
a month for their lodging.

Not until 1925, after many petitions, did we succeed in getting permission to use Teliatinki, the estate that had once belonged to Chertkov. It had become an orphan asylum after the
Revolution.

It makes me shudder to think of this place. I had often heard
about it before I saw it. One of the teachers came to me several
times, asking for a position. She was a nervous girl, with a
twitching face, and her black eyes seemed always frightened.
She told me that the director—a Communist—violated the girls
in the home, and that some of them, children of fourteen, were
pregnant. I did not believe her, but later I met his successor
(the orphanage was moved to another estate when we took
over Teliatinki). She complained that the government did not
give her money enough to run the home and feed the orphans,
much less the babies that the girls had. "It's lucky," she added,
"that the girls get alimony."[3]

When I visited Teliatinki I found a number of children
roaming about the dark kitchen barefoot and in rags, but with
fur caps on their heads. It was terribly cold in the house. The
children were dirty, and their look of fear struck me. Behind a
stove, in a filthy corner, a boy was hiding. One of the teachers
went up to him and said something. The boy did not answer; I
saw the blade of a kitchen knife sparkle in the shadow.

Chairs and windows were broken, the air was stale and close,

[3] According to Soviet law, if a woman, married or unmarried, can prove the iden-
tity of the father of her child, she receives part of his wages for its support.

the children paid no attention whatever to the teachers, and it was plain at once that they were out of all control. Vagrancy seemed no worse than such a seminary of dirt and corruption, and the children could not have been worse off in the streets, where the air at least was fresh.

Such was the Teliatinki place when we got it from the Provincial Board of Education. The walls were falling in, the roofs leaked, every window pane was broken, there was dirt everywhere. The plumbing was out of order, there was no running water and no toilet in the house, and the children, not wanting to go outside, had used the attic for a toilet.

We spent several months getting the money to repair the place: to rebuild and clean the house, put the plumbing in order, install electricity, and plant vegetable gardens. There were several houses on the estate. We moved the seven-year industrial school and the orphanage to Teliatinki.

XLIV

THE WAIFS

CHILDREN were buzzing around me like flies about a dish of honey. One of them shoved me. They probably wanted my briefcase, but I did not think they would risk snatching it out of my hands. The street was full of people, and on the corner a policeman was standing. At night, in lonely streets, the urchins often stole bags and purses but not in the daytime. I walked on, trying to pay no attention to the boys around me, holding fast to my briefcase. They followed me. Annoyed, I turned to the policeman.

"These children are bothering me! I have important papers in my bag and I am afraid they are trying to get it."

The man smiled. "That's not what they want. Look, you're losing your fountain pen!"

I looked down and saw that my pen had almost been pulled out of my breast pocket. Fountain pens were scarce in Moscow. They could not be bought in the stores, and mine was a present from American friends. I took it out of my pocket and put it into the briefcase. The boys stopped following me, except for one who ran ahead of me, climbed on a post, and stuck out his tongue.

There were crowds of waifs in Moscow in summer. They roamed the streets, stealing and begging, and slept in the tanks in which asphalt was made. As soon as autumn came, like the birds, they made their way south. They got rides on trains, hiding under the benches or in the boxes under the cars. At big stations, they would come out of their hiding places and beg for bread. Sometimes the conductors threw them off the train, and then they would wait for the next one; but usually no one paid any attention to them.

My summer vacation trip to the Caucasus often took me to Tuapse. The town was full of vagrants, and there I once saw a waif begging:

"Citizen, give me a kopek! A cigarette!"

"You are too young to smoke," the gentleman said. "Where are your parents?"

The boy scowled, impervious to the sentimental remarks of grown-ups.

"Go and wash your face," the gentleman continued. "It is bad for little boys like you to be so dirty. You'll have a rash. Look at yourself. You're as black as a negro . . ."

"Give me five kopeks and I'll wash myself!"

"You really ought to be clean for your own sake . . . but, well, all right . . ."

The boy picked up a watermelon peel, broke it in half, and began rubbing his face. Streams of soot-blackened juice ran down his neck. From under the black mask, a smiling, white, childish face appeared.

"Give me the kopeks."

The gentleman sighed and took out his purse.

"Give me five kopeks and I'll wash my face, too," a girl about eight years old suggested.

"Is this your sister?" the gentleman asked.

"No, she's my wife!"

In the daytime the children begged; at night they stole. There was always a crowd of people in the station at Tuapse waiting for a train, and sometimes when the conductor asked for the tickets on the platform someone would put down his bag. Then a hook would fasten swiftly on to the handle and it would slide away under the train.

Once when I was returning to Yasnaia Poliana with three companions, we had to wait a long time for our tickets in Tuapse. It was very crowded and close in the station. We got a kettle of boiling water and had tea on the porch near the front door. For some reason or without any reason, this door was locked. Only several broken windows were gaping into the dark. At first we were alone, but presently a group of boys appeared.

"Tim ta ti-ra-ra-ra! Tim ta ra! Tim ta ti-ra-ra!"

One of them was singing and dancing. We could not see his

face, but his movements were graceful, and the rhythm of the dancing and singing was wonderful.

"What a devil!" one of the boys exclaimed with admiration. "Isn't he smart!"

"Madlenka isn't here—the two of them would show you!"

"Madlenka is making love to the red-haired . . ."

The dancer stopped short and turned on him.

"You dirty beast! If that's true, if she . . . I'll break every one of her ribs!"

"Tim ta ti-ra-ra-ra! Tim ta ra!"

Suddenly the singing and dancing stopped. A broad-shouldered man ran up the steps.

"Hurry!" He bent over the smallest lad and whispered something in his ear. Then, with a quick movement he lifted him, putting his right arm around his chest and holding his feet with his left, and let him down into the station through the broken window. No one spoke. We could see cigarettes glowing in the dark. From the city park came the sound of music— the same tune that the boy had been singing.

Suddenly something fell through the window. The little boy landed flat on his hands and knees. He was sobbing.

"O little Uncle," he gasped, "the guard caught me! I just got away . . ."

"And you didn't get it . . . Ah! . . ."

The man swore.

ONE day after school I found a boy sitting on the porch at Yasnaia Poliana.

"What do you want?"

"I want the woman that takes care of orphans. Her name's Tolstoy."

"Are you an orphan?"

"Yes."

"Where have you come from?"

"I am a waif. I was going to my grandmother. The conductor caught me and put me off the train at Yasnaia Poliana.

They told me there that this Tolstoy woman was taking care of orphans."

"How about stealing? Know something about it?"

"No, I begged—I never stole."

"All right, we'll see."

I sent him to the steam bath and then to the farm-workers' room, and told them to keep an eye on him. After two weeks, I asked the workers about him. They liked him. He was polite, helpful, and seemed to be honest.

Volodia was taken into the orphans' dormitory, and there, too, both teachers and students liked him. He was a good student and showed some talent for drawing. During a year and a half, no one ever complained of him. Everybody forgot that he was a boy from the street, until early one morning a teacher came to me from the dormitory at Teliatinki. He looked very upset.

"Do you know what's happened?" he said. "Volodia has run away."

"When?"

"In the middle of the night. He stole seven rubles from the boys and three pairs of new boots."

We telephoned to the police and to the railway stations, but Volodia was not to be found.

At first the boys would tell us nothing; then, gradually, it came out that Volodia had been reading Jack London all winter. He had talked about going away, traveling . . . and when the spring came, he could not bear it any longer. He missed the free life he had led all his childhood, and he left.

XLV

BADGERING

WHEN the Yasnaia Poliana project was approved by the Central Executive Committee, one of the members said: "I think we can afford the luxury of having one Tolstoy nest in the Soviet Union."

I never forgot this sentence. I built my whole work on it. I repeated it to everyone who would listen. I tried to hammer it into the minds of all the local Communists, and when they spread the usual Soviet propaganda in Yasnaia Poliana, I said, "Do you know that even the Central Executive Committee has said that the Soviet Government can afford the luxury of having one Tolstoy nest in the Soviet Union?" I repeated it to the Department of Education, to the members of the Central Executive Committee themselves, who had, no doubt, long ago forgotten this casual remark. My tone was so firm that it never occurred to the Communists to contradict me. We worked comparatively unmolested for more than three years.

Yasnaia Poliana was very independent. When an agent of the trade-union came from Tula and tried to collect money for military purposes, we refused to give any. "Tolstoy was a pacifist," we said. "We do our work in his name and cannot support military organizations."

The Tula authorities were worried and held meetings to discuss Yasnaia Poliana. But these did not bother us.

The persecution began quite unexpectedly. In the newspaper *Pravda* an article appeared, asserting that a former countess and other members of the bourgeoisie were living in Yasnaia Poliana! "Secluding themselves on the estate, these bourgeois are holding to their old practices; they have orgies, they make the museum janitors serve them and keep the samovars lighted all night long; and as a reward for a night's work, they throw them the crumbs from their table. To disguise all this, Alexandra Tolstoy has organized an agricultural coöperative. She is president of the organization and gets most of the profit from the farm. The employees are not paid; they go hungry, and are often dismissed without any reason. The school teaches religion. The children know nothing about the revolutionary holidays."

Cars came from the city nearly every day. One inspection followed another. The farm was inspected, the office, the museum, the schools. Communists found fault with everything and threatened to have all of us dismissed. Strangers went over the estate, the fields and gardens, the schools. Paying no attention whatever to the administrators of Yasnaia Poliana, they talked with the employees and the students.

"Maria Petrovna, Maria Petrovna!" a rosy-cheeked fellow in the sixth class shouted to the teacher of physics: "I'll tell you something! Did you see that dark man in school today? The one that is around all the time now? Do you know what he asked me?"

"What?"

"He asked me if the teachers spanked us. And do you know what I said? 'Sure . . . they do.'" The boy waited for a moment to see the effect of his words. "'They spank us every day,' I said, 'especially the teacher of physics, she's wicked . . .'"

Dark clouds were gathering around Yasnaia Poliana. Every time we heard the sound of a car coming up the drive, our hearts sank.

"Mamma, mamma!" my three-year-old grandniece shouted, "again motobiles have alived, the wicked uncles have alived!" She knew that no one except the "wicked uncles" could come in an automobile.

According to custom, every summer we had a "forest holiday," when we planted trees around our new school building, and then had a picnic for all the children. In the spring of 1924, the Forest Department of the Commissariat of Agriculture arranged a similar holiday for the population in our neighborhood, and invited the peasants of Yasnaia Poliana to take part in it. The head of the Forest Department, a young Communist, delivered a speech. At first he talked of the usefulness of trees; then he began to speak about Yasnaia Poliana:

"Citizens! It is time for us to get rid of all the counterrevolutionary elements that are hiding away in warm corners under pretext of working for our country. Right there," and he pointed toward the high trees of the park at Yasnaia Poliana, rising above the apple orchard, "on this very estate, all the bourgeois exploiters have found a refuge with this rascal Tolstoy at their head! Citizens! You must help us in our struggle . . ." and so on.

I do not think that such speeches impressed the old peasants, but they certainly affected the younger ones, instilling a hostile feeling toward us in their ignorant minds.

Cherniavsky, the "dark man," who was the director of the Communist school in Tula, was trying to influence not only the peasants and students, but our employees, too. The janitors, coachmen, and farm-workers would still obey me, but they paid no attention to my assistants and the teachers. They not only ignored their orders but were rude to them. Once when a teacher had to go to Moscow to a conference and told the coachman to harness the horse to take him to the station, the man shouted angrily: "No more tsarist *régime* now! If you want to go, harness the horse yourself!"

The local Communists with Cherniavsky as their leader built a club house on the outskirts of the village, just opposite the estate, to forward Marxism, militarism, and antireligious propaganda among the peasants. In sign of derision they set it facing north, so that the back, ornamented with a small wooden toilet, faced toward the estate of Yasnaia Poliana.

At night gangs of young peasants came to the park, and cut inscriptions on the benches, broke the trees, and left the paths littered with paper and sunflower seeds. Sometimes these fellows would come to our windows and curse us on behalf of the Yasnaia Poliana inhabitants. Auntie would start up in bed, eager to drive them out and punish them. I had to beg her to be quiet. She could never really understand the new situation, and I was afraid that with her fiery temper she might make things worse.

The continued restraint of my indignation made me literally ill. But I knew that I could only win by being patient. One reckless word could ruin not only me but the whole organization. There was one hope of salvation, and that was Moscow.

Kalinin listened. He did not say he believed me. It looked to me as if the local Communists had been getting in their word with the Central Executive Committee itself.

"I will make an investigation," he said.

Time went on and the atmosphere at Yasnaia Poliana grew more charged every day. Many of our teachers had had the experience before of seeing their schools destroyed by ignorant local Communists. Everybody was upset. We discussed the situation repeatedly, trying to find a way out, and at the same time continued to work feverishly. One of my assistants was fighting for Yasnaia Poliana at a teachers' conference in Tula; another was helping me to write a report of our school activity. Sometimes we worked until three o'clock in the morning trying to get our reports ready for the inspection.

The continuous necessity of restraining my anger, the feeling of helplessness and injustice weighed on me so heavily that my heart began to bother me. One night I felt very sick and went to bed. I had hardly closed my eyes when there was a knock at the door.

"Come in!"

A group of teachers entered the study.

"What is the matter?"

"A meeting is going on in the park. Comrade Cherniavsky has been demonstrating an antireligious movie and now he is talking and persuading the young people to destroy all the bourgeois in Yasnaia Poliana. The young men are excited. They have torn up all the saplings . . ."

Again an unsteady feeling in my heart and a lump in my throat . . .

"We can't bear it any longer!" one of the teachers said.

"Something has got to be done. We can't live under the constant threat of being driven out or put in prison . . ."

"We can't do anything," I said. "We must wait patiently for the committee of inquiry of the Central Executive Committee."

"It will never come . . ." I heard one of the teachers pace up and down the dark room. "But in the meantime they'll ruin our work."

"ALEXANDRA LVOVNA! Alexandra Lvovna!" shouted one of the teachers, rushing into my office. "Quick, the committee! An automobile full of people."

"Where?"

"Under the elm tree—five or six! Please take this school bulletin. Show them that the revolutionary holidays have all been observed."

As I hurried toward the front door, other employees nearly rushed me off my feet.

"The investigating committee! Comrade Cherniavsky is with them!"

Six people were getting out of a big car: the President of the Tula Provincial Executive Committee, the head of the Tula Department of Education, the head of the Workers' Inspection of Tula, Comrade Cherniavsky, and two members of the Central Executive Committee.

This was a serious affair. Everybody knew it. The employees were summoned, and I was asked to leave the room. In about an hour I was called into the office.

"Alexandra Lvovna," Comrade Kiselev of the Central Executive Committee said, "what share do you get from your farm?"

Instead of answering, I asked the bookkeeper, who was present, to give me the books of the coöperative. I showed one of the entries to Kiselev. It stated that, having no time to work in the fields now because of school and museum work, Citizen Tolstoy refused to take her share of the proceeds from the farm.

"Hm! Now allow me to ask you: When did you have a banquet with wine that lasted until morning?"

"On the twenty-third of April. It was my name day."

"How many persons were there?"

"About forty."

"How much wine did you have?"

"Two bottles of port."

The members of the committee looked at each other and smiled.

"Is Citizen Tolstoy telling us the truth?" they asked the janitor, Tolkach, who, as I understood, was one of the most important witnesses against me.

"Well, I guess she is."

"Did you have the janitor Tolkach work for you until two o'clock in the morning, making him heat the samovars?"

"No, that was . . ."

"Didn't Tolkach light the samovar for you at two in the morning?"

"Yes, he did, but I will tell you how that happened, and Tolkach will correct me if I am mistaken. That was on the twenty-third of April. Tolkach was on night duty. I invited him to join our party and have tea with us. He seemed pleased, joined us, sang songs with us. At two o'clock in the morning, my assistant, seeing that the samovar was empty, started for the kitchen to have it refilled. He couldn't ask the janitor, who was our invited guest, to do it for us. But Tolkach was very nice about it. He got up, took the samovar and heated it himself, and he was the first to get a cup of hot tea . . ."

"Is that right, Comrade Tolkach?"

"Ye . . ."

"Comrade Tolkach told me about the incident from a somewhat different point of view," Cherniavsky interrupted.

"When the party was over, about three, I thought of Tolkach's wife and children, wrapped up some apple pie and candy and handed them to Tolkach. I hadn't the slightest intention of offending him, and he did not seem to take it that way."

The questioning lasted for more than an hour and when it was over, I asked permission to speak. I was rewarded at last for several months of patient silence, and suddenly I became the accuser. I told the members of the Central Executive Committee how Cherniavsky tried to undermine the discipline of the students and the employees; how, under his influence, the park was being destroyed; how he took for his confederates the worst and the most dishonest of the peasants and employees and it was they who had been witnesses against us. Anger made me eloquent. Cherniavsky turned red and pale. Several times he tried to interrupt.

"Allow me . . ."

"No, we have listened to you enough," an inspector said. "Now we are going to listen to Alexandra Lvovna."

And when at last the inquiry was over, the Tula officials were asked to leave the room and I stayed alone with the members of the Central Executive Committee.

"What do you want us to do?" they asked.

"I want a retraction of the newspaper article," I said, "and a chance to work."

They promised it.

The officials from Tula tried to make me dismiss two of my assistants. I refused, and they let them stay.

Accidentally or not, the administration of Tula changed. A new director of the Department of Education was appointed; Comrade Cherniavsky also disappeared.

The incident of the inquiry made it plain to the local administrators that the persecution of the intelligentsia was not to be practiced at Yasnaia Poliana, and the local Communists became more careful, but their dislike did not diminish.

XLVI

AUCTION!

PETERSBURG reminded me of Pompeii, with its cold, empty temples, deserted palaces, barren stores. I roamed about the streets, and a feeling of bitterness for the beautiful half-dead city tormented me. Memories slipped one after another through my mind—of the broad and animated Nevsky Prospect, the grand "Strelka," where day and night elegant carriages and automobiles passed; the Alexandrine Theater, and ladies sparkling with jewels, and officers in gold and silver braid; the Winter Palace, and my strict but wonderful great aunt who was lady-in-waiting to the Tsarina; policemen saluting us when she took me in her carriage; visits; the eternal arguing between young people as to which was better, Moscow or Petersburg; youthful sorrows, white sleepless nights, my first unreturned love.

The Yasnaia Poliana librarian and I were in Petersburg to get some books for our library, for the largest supply was there. Books had been collected from private homes; some of them might have come from the Tsar's library. There were many thousands of them piled up in an enormous warehouse, where a few people from the Commissariat of Education were trying to classify and catalogue them. Among the piles, we found old rare things, such as copies of the magazine *Sovremennik,* founded and edited by Pushkin. We went through the materials in the warehouse every day until three; then we walked about the city.

With the feeling you have when in the midst of ruin you discover a beautiful vase unbroken, I entered the apartment where Pushkin lived. This was now a museum, cared for by people like myself, and furnished in the old mode. There was peace and dignity here.

The Tolstoy Museum gave the same impression. For scant wages, a few devoted people were endeavoring to preserve here the relics of Russian art, science, and culture. The workers in the Tolstoy Museum had spent years collecting manuscripts, clippings, portraits, pictures. Now there was a possibility that the museum might be done away with. It was under the auspices of the Academy of Science, but the academy had no money to keep it up.

We wanted to see the Winter Palace. It was closed, but as we crossed the square, we saw a few people hurrying in that direction. They seemed to have a definite objective. We followed them. They did not go under the arch into the palace, but turned to the right into a dark hall where a dim lamp was burning. People were crowding around a man behind a table.

"Fifty!" he shouted. "Fifty once, fifty twice . . ."

"What is this?" I asked a woman who stood near me.

"What? Don't you see? They are selling what's left of the Tsar's things."

"Fifty-five once, fifty-five . . ."

Lamp mantels, faded fans, cups, dishes, ribbons, brooms, and a number of empty cases with the inscription: "To his Imperial Majesty Nicholas II . . ." By the round and oval holes in the beautiful leather cases, I thought they must once have held silver or gold dishes.

"Where are the contents of those cases?" a woman beside me sighed.

"Where?" an elderly man retorted sharply. "Where? Surely 'the masters' have got them . . ."

Nobody wanted to buy a straw hat with a plain blue ribbon on it priced at ten kopeks. I wondered to whom that had belonged. To a young girl? Was she still alive? But all the cases were sold. A group of men in long greasy overcoats were bidding for them.

"They want the leather," someone said.

"A real Dresden ware dish!" the man at the counter shouted. "Three rubles!"

"Three-fifty!" I cried.

"Three-fifty-five!"

"Four!"

I stuck to it and got it for seven rubles.

"Dust cloths! Ten kopeks!" The auctioneer pulled from under the counter a handful of dirty rags.

"Fifteen kopeks!" a woman called, and became the owner of the pile.

"It's fine, isn't it, to use the Tsar's dirty rags in your home?" the elderly man said.

"Six goblets belonging to Paul I! Fifteen rubles!"

"Sixteen!" I cried.

On the green crystal sparkled the gold monogram of Tsar Paul and the Imperial crown. The goblets were of an unusual antique shape and very beautiful.

"Seventeen!" someone shouted.

"Seventeen!" repeated the auctioneer, and, very quickly, "seventeen once, twice, three times!"

I lost the goblets.

"They know what costs money," the old man said. "Those went to one of their own."

We left the palace silently. It was already dark. Damp snow was falling abundantly.

I took the Dresden dish home. I liked to look at it. The roses were beautiful and there was the Tsar's crown at the bottom. When I touched it with my finger, it gave a clear ring. But I felt uneasy. The people to whom the dish had belonged were tortured and killed . . . and it had been stolen from them.

XLVII

"COMRADES"

COMRADE PANOV was president of the district Soviet. Under the provisional government, he had been a conscientious member of the Tula police. He was the kind who is always devoted to the people who give him a job. Panov reminded me of a small dog, a mongrel with Boston terrier blood. He had the rolling eyes and protruding forehead of a Boston terrier and like them was sometimes nasty but never courageous. He shaved his head, which was nearly the same color as his pale greenish face, and tried to look like a gentleman, in new clothes and shiny boots. He was always the first to hold out his weak, dirty, white hand, rigid, and cold as a toad. To appear well educated he used foreign words which he did not understand himself, and sometimes we could hardly keep from laughing when he spoke. He enjoyed his own importance enormously.

"May I use your telephone?"

"Yes, Comrade Panov."

"Hallo, hallo! Department of Education! I want to speak to the president. Panov, the President of the Shchokinsky Soviet, speaking. We need teachers! We are suffering immensely from the lack of pedagogical personalities! Number? How many? We need six personalities!"

He would come into the classes and speak to the students. "How about religion, comrades? Are you going to church? Are you poisoning yourself with the drugs of religious prejudices?"

Panov insisted on our having Communists in the faculty of the school. We argued that the Tolstoy school did not need Communists.

"You are a counterrevolutionist, Comrade Tolstoy!" he told me.

"And if I were, what would you do?" I laughed.

Suddenly he looked straight into my face. The terrier's upper lip lifted in a snarl. He clenched his weak, pale hands.

"What? I'd shoot you!" he whispered. "If only I could prove what you are, I'd shoot you, shoot you without pity, with my own hand!"

Moscow also insisted on our having a Communist in the school.

"Who is doing the political work? Who is teaching political grammar?" they asked me.

I tried to avoid the question, but it was repeated again and again. At last, in 1925, the director of the Department of Experimental Schools insisted upon sending out a Communist to teach political grammar.

I was anxious. Whom would they pick? A person who never had heard the name of Tolstoy, who would not understand our work, and who would introduce Marxist propaganda, set up "godless corners" in school, teach militarism, perhaps denounce us to the Communist cell? A number of schools had been demoralized by Communists who, supported by the local committee, had become dictators of the establishments. Every Communist, even if sent from the center, was under the control of the local Communists, and we knew them too well not to be disquieted.

The Communist came one morning. I decided to speak to her at once. I outlined my father's ideas, and told her that our school had no military training and no antireligious propaganda; that even the members of the Central Executive Committee, in honor of my father, did not insist on our fighting against religion. I hoped that notwithstanding her communistic ideas she would understand us. I trusted in her tact . . .

As I went on talking, I felt a little uneasy. I was ready to meet opposition, arguments, the self-confidence that usually characterizes the members of the ruling party. Instead I met perplexed brown eyes, and the girl's kind, good-natured face, ravaged by smallpox, expressed only embarrassment. She smiled, showing bad teeth, and was absolutely silent.

In school, special hours were set for classes in political grammar. The new Communist teacher was supposed to give a report of her work in teachers' meeting. But when, as chairman of the meeting, I called on her, she said that her report was not ready. It was not ready at the second meeting either, and I had to reprove her. When this happened a third time, Comrade Malvina simply covered her face with her hands and sobbed:

"Please leave me alone, won't you?"

The poor girl did not know anything about teaching or writing reports.

Fortunately, later on, political grammar was included in the course in so-called Social Science, which was taught in the schools instead of history. I appointed Comrade Malvina librarian, very glad to have such a harmless, "tame Communist" in the organization.

But Malvina got too tame. We corrupted her with our ideas. Once, as I was coming out of the museum, I met her on the porch.

"I want to speak to you," she said, and burst into tears.

"Well, what's the matter? Has something happened?" I asked.

Sobbing like a child, she told me that she could no longer belong to the party.

"Why?" I asked. It flashed through my mind that if Malvina should leave the party, I would lose my "tame Communist," and another one would be sent to us. "Why, Malvina? Don't you want to be a member of the party?"

"I can't, Alexandra Lvovna! If only you knew how mean they are! They make us denounce you and say all kinds of bad things about you, and spy . . . No, no, I can't stay with them any more. Oh, tell me what to do!"

Her grief was so real that I forgot my own worries, and forgot to make fun of her as I always had.

"Malvina," I asked her, "tell me the truth. Do you believe in the work of the Communist party as you did before?"

"Well . . . no," she said. "I don't. Maybe I still believe in socialism, but not in the Bolshevik party . . ."

"Then, Malvina, you cannot be a member."

"Thank you," she said, "I knew you would tell me that. I will go to the cell and tell them today."

Poor Malvina! As soon as she lost her membership, she lost almost everything else. She went from one job to another until at last she became an under clerk in an office, and even this work she did badly.

OUR next Communist was a member of the Komsomol.[1] She was sent from Moscow in 1927 as the leader of the Young Pioneers. Comrade Alexandrova lived at Teliatinki and taught the second grade of the primary school. Luckily this girl was also too stupid to be harmful. She was a plump, rosy-cheeked, lazy, sleepy creature. The only subject that aroused her was sex. Everyone in the school made fun of her.

"Which do you like better: the instructor of the workshops or the bookkeeper?" the teachers would ask her.

Alexandrova opened her red lips, her small gray eyes shone.

"Ivan Stepanovich is a real man, and I love men like that. He is so big and strong, and well built . . . the bookkeeper is too gentle, too refined . . ."

Everyone laughed, and I was happy that we had another harmless member of the party. But soon rumors were heard that the "Komsomolka" had received several men during one night. And the tutors insisted upon her leaving Teliatinki when they learned that she had made love to some of the older boys in the orphan home.

For several months, I could not get rid of the girl. Not until the director of the Department of Experimental Schools, who sent her to us, was discharged, did I succeed in dismissing her.

AT first there was no Komsomol cell at Yasnaia Poliana. Then the Tula cell started one, and the number of Komsomols among the students increased rapidly because those who wished

[1] The Komsomol is the Union of Communist youth in Soviet Russia. It is regarded as a school of Communism and its task is to train the future leaders of the country. The age limits for the membership are from 14 to 23.

to go on to the university were obliged to join in order to be admitted.

"WHAT shall we do with Katia?" the teachers were saying. "She misses her classes, or when she goes, she is sulky and rude and won't do anything."

I talked to Katia and to her parents. In many ways Katia was our best pupil. She was capable and when she studied did well in class. We had been proud of her. Now, what was wrong?

At last we found out. Katia was going to have a baby.

This had never happened in the school before. Everybody was excited. Who was the father of the child? So far as we knew, there had been no relations between the boys and girls in the school. Later we learned that the father was Vorobiev, the secretary of the Komsomol cell, who had been sent from the Tula cell to be the leader of our youngsters.

ONE night a pretty seventeen-year-old girl came to my room. She was in the highest class, was to be graduated that year and continue her education in the university. Two years before, she had joined the Komsomol, for unless she did, she could not continue her studies.

She was very upset and could hardly keep from crying.

"What is the matter, Marina?"

"I'm lost, Alexandra Lvovna!"

"Why?"

"I've been expelled from the Komsomol."

"What for?"

"Comrade Vorobiev has reported that my father was an employee of the old police . . ."

"But they knew it before, didn't they?"

"Yes, but they paid no attention to it. My father was a clerk in the police office. He was not a policeman. But now Vorobiev is angry . . ."

"Why?"

The girl blushed and lowered her eyes: "He made love to me, and I sent him off . . . I hate him . . ."

The next day I spoke to Vorobiev. The boy was impudent. I went to the secretary of the Tula cell and begged him to help Marina. The secretary refused. Marina was expelled from the Komsomol. She was graduated from our school, but she could not go to the university, and, as a daughter of a police employee, and disfranchised, could not become a member of the trade-union and get a job.

For a year I lost sight of Marina. Then one day as I was walking through the main street of Tula someone called to me, "Alexandra Lvovna!"

"Marina!"

She was as good looking as ever, but her face and lips were painted.

"How do you do, Alexandra Lvovna."

"I am glad to see you, Marina. Where are you living now? Are you working?" Marina did not answer. She turned away her handsome head and wept.

XLVIII

SCHOOL PROBLEMS

THE "complex method," which called for tying all subjects to a central theme, was a great puzzle to the teachers. A country school teacher with meager education had to abandon the routine he had followed all his life. Instead of teaching reading, writing, and arithmetic to eight-year-olds, he was ordered to discuss with them the aims and purposes of the October Revolution, and the changes that followed. To this discussion, he had to link arithmetic, spelling, and drawing. It was no wonder that he often did not understand what was expected of him. In vain the inspectors drove from one school to another and called conferences and meetings.

There were no textbooks for arithmetic. The teacher had to invent the problems. Here is an example of a problem on the achievements of October:

"Before the Revolution a kulak owned 5 cows and 12 sheep. After the Revolution, 3 cows and 7 sheep were taken away from him. How many cows and sheep did he have left?"

Sometimes absurd things happened. In one of the annual reports, a teacher from Siberia stated that while working out the complex "domestic animals" he had succeeded in tying everything up with "the cow" except music.

At a teachers' conference in Tula I heard a conversation between two teachers:

"We were working on the complex 'cat,'" one of them said. "Well, I succeeded in connecting spelling and arithmetic . . ."

"How did you tie up arithmetic with the cat?"

"Oh, that was easy enough, we measured the cats' tails."

FOR a whole winter, the seventh-year students experimented with feeding cattle by using the so-called Danish system, under the direction of the teacher of agriculture. The boys cared for the cows belonging to several peasants. They wrote down the ration and the amount of milk the animals gave, and at the same time they observed a few cows that were fed by peasants in the usual way. The experiment turned out very well. The peasants whose cows were fed by the Danish system began selling their milk. Other peasants, anxious to imitate the results, asked the boys to give them the same feed for their cows.

At a meeting in the club house the students demonstrated their method with short talks and diagrams. The peasants were pleased; but it seemed strange to me that none of the farmers whose cows had given such brilliant results under the Danish system was present.

"Where are the owners of the cows?" I asked one of the peasants.

"Oh, they are at home," he answered.

"Why? They ought to be more interested than anyone else."

"Well," the man answered, "of course they are. Nikolai Orekhov told me that he earned nearly a hundred rubles a month from his two cows. But you see they are afraid. If the officials learn how much milk they sell, they'll have to pay high taxes and they may be denounced as kulaks; and, who knows, their cows may be taken away from them; so they think they'd better sit quietly at home . . ."

WHILE the professor from Moscow was sipping his tea, the teachers surrounded him, eager to hear what the learned man would say.

"We cannot guarantee that the first experiment will give us astonishing results . . ." he began.

One of the teachers coughed into his hand and moved nearer to the table, so as not to miss a word.

"But, comrades, if you will concentrate all your attention on the experiment and help me, we shall get good results and lay the foundation for a very interesting piece of work. It will not only have practical results for your schools, but it may also be of some scientific value to our Experimental Institute . . ."

"Do you think that there is a great difference in the psychology of the country and the city children? . . . Another sandwich?"

"Thank you. Yes, the excitability of the city children is greater. But psychological tests give wonderful results—and, if we could collaborate with your school, we could study the village children to better advantage."

"How wonderful that would be! We are isolated from the civilized world, from modern ideas in pedagogy . . ."

The dean was not a Communist, but she was considered a good teacher. She knew that collaboration with the Moscow Experimental Institute would raise the reputation of our school and help her standing as well.

"Are you very tired, professor?" she asked, "or may we start the tests today?"

"We will begin at once. Let me see, we'll take the third grade."

"The third? You are beginning with my class?" exclaimed an elderly teacher, her face going a splotchy red.

"We will begin with the third grade," the professor repeated, ignoring her agitation. "Every pupil must have a clean sheet of paper and a well-sharpened pencil. Don't excite the children; they must be as calm as if they were having an ordinary lesson."

And the professor, followed by the dean and several other teachers, left the room.

"Katerina Petrovna, Katerina Petrovna!" the old lady whispered, catching the dean in the corridor. "What shall I do? I haven't got any paper. I can't use the scraps that we brought from the office the other day!"

"Don't fidget like that, I'll give you paper," the dean said as she hurried away.

The school hummed like a beehive. The bell rang, and the children, pushing, laughing, and talking, went to their classes.

"God help me!" the elderly teacher breathed, making the sign of the cross under her coat.

"Don't be nervous, Tatiana Andreyevna!" one of the teachers said as they met in the doorway. "I won't mind a bit if he comes to my class!"

"I'm not nervous!" Tatiana Andreyevna retorted. "I've been teaching children twenty-six years, and they've never made any mistakes in their spelling after the four years of the primary school, and now, with these new methods and tests of theirs, the students who've been through the nine-year school make seventy mistakes on one page!"

"Tatiana Andreyevna!" the children shouted when she entered, "is the professor going to test us?"

"Is he very severe?"

"What will we have, arithmetic?"

" 'Goldy' is pinching me! Ouch!"

Suddenly there was absolute silence. The professor entered, followed by the dean and several of the high school teachers.

"Good morning!"

Thirty young heads turned toward him, thirty pairs of bright eyes examined the little man: "Good morning!"

"Distribute the pencils and paper!" he told the teacher. "Now be calm. This is just a lesson like every day. We must all be calm and quiet."

He explained how they were to do the work, and then suddenly shouted:

"Silence! No more questions! Concentrate on your work! One, two, three! Elbows on your desk!"

The children did not move. Some of them, smiling bashfully, put their pencils in their mouths, others stared at the professor, some looked up at their teacher for help.

"Your elbows like this!" shouted the professor. "Get ready to start. Every second counts! One, two, three!"

This was a test in attention and speed. One after another the children handed their work in. At last every one of them was through, except a little chap with a rosy face and blue eyes who was still scratching out figures. The professor was ready to start another test; the boy was still writing.

"What are you doing?" the dean asked. "Why are you so long?"

"Oh," he said, "I am looking it over again. I don't want to have any mistakes at all."

"Well, it isn't my fault if the children fail," said a young teacher, a Komsomol. "What can I do? It's the bad influence of the parents, those kulaks . . ."

"You are a bad Communist, that's all," someone laughed. "Let's see the question. 'Whom does the Red Army defend— the government, the working class, or the bourgeoisie?' The answer is 'the government.' That's not bad. 'Who are the enemies of the people—the bourgeoisie, the Bolsheviks?' Oh, Comrade Alexandrova, this is a splendid example of your communistic influence! Look, one, two, three children have answered 'the Bolsheviks.' "

"Oh, leave me alone!" the young girl exclaimed. "I wish the damned tests had never been invented."

"Never mind. Those tests of yours won't go into the annual report! Let's see: 'What must you take with you to a coöperative?' 'A bag.' Well, that's not bad. You certainly need a bag to bring your things home. 'Money.' That sounds reasonable, too. 'As much bread as you can.' I don't see that. Why bread?"

"Oh, one of the pupils explained that to me. She said they usually had to go to the coöperative and stand in line from two or three in the morning till eight, so that they get very hungry."

"How funny! And what was the answer supposed to be?"

"Well, I don't know who wrote those tests, but they're no use to us. The answer is supposed to be 'your food card.' Of course you need a food card, but you need a bag and bread and money, too—they don't give you credit."

Seriozha Khokhlov, an orphan of fifteen, gave the best answers on political questions, but in mathematics he was scarcely better than a child of eight. He had not been promoted, and was not ready to be, but he was too big for his class. We found him a job as a painter in Tula.

"How dare you put me out?" Seriozha shouted. "I am a Komsomol, a member of the party. You want to fill your school with bourgeois sprouts like ——!" And he called out the names of the teachers' children. "I'm a real proletarian."

The boy was so bold that I wondered if someone had given him instructions. He had never been like this before.

"You'll remember me though!" he shouted as he left the school.

"Who were those people who came yesterday in a car?" I asked a teacher.

"I don't know. They said they were appointed overseers of the orphan home. They brought presents for the children, and held a meeting with the Komsomols and the Pioneers. I was not allowed to be present . . ."

"You ought to have sent them to me," I said.

"I tried to, but they paid no attention. I couldn't stop them . . ."

"Telephone me immediately if they come again."

A few days later the same teacher came to Yasnaia Poliana to talk with me.

"I can't do anything with the children," he said. "They are getting disorderly. Seriozha used to be their leader; now it's Vania. He goes about complaining that they get bad food and poor clothes. At meals they all make a racket, shouting that their food is stale; they throw spoons about."

"Someone has been telling them to do that. How about those people who came last week?"

"They came again. I telephoned to you, you were in Moscow."

Several days passed. Late one evening the telephone rang.

"Those people from Tula are here. They have brought the children candy and clothes and they've got them all together now in a meeting."

The children were gathered in the assembly hall when I arrived, and a man in a khaki uniform and a woman were on the platform. They stopped talking when I entered.

"We are having a private talk with the children," the man said.

"I am the director of the school."

"But this is a party meeting."

"All right, but before you continue your meeting, I want to know who you are and who gave you permission to come into the school without even speaking to the director."

The man did not answer. He handed me a paper from the government which stated that the Tula branch of the G.P.U. was to supervise the Yasnaia Poliana Orphan Home.

"THE Yasnaia Poliana school is one of those bourgeois schools that must be destroyed without the slightest pity. All the teachers in the school are bourgeois and counterrevolutionists; some of them are the sons and daughters of priests.

"Children are beaten in the school. The food is bad. The dormitory food is mixed with worms, glass, and roaches.

"Comrades, watch this hydra of counterrevolution!"

The article was signed "Invisible."

Seriozha Khokhlov came to Teliatinki on an assignment from the local government newspaper, for which he was correspondent, to investigate the conditions in the Orphan Home. I told the teachers to turn him out. He went as far as the yard, where he began firing a gun in the air and yelling. A few boys belonging to the Komsomol joined him, and then they held a meeting.

"Comrades!" the next article by "Invisible" asked: "When will this damned aristocracy be choked? When shall we clear the way for building up our socialist country? . . ."

More inspections. More officials from Moscow.

XLIX

CHIPS FLY WHEN WOOD IS CHOPPED

"MAY I speak to the acting commissar?"

"Just a moment, please. I'll ask."

The secretary gathered some papers from the table and put them into a folder marked "For Signature." Then he disappeared into the office of the Acting Commissar of Education, Epstein.

"Yes, in about half an hour."

With a politeness not at all characteristic of the Komsomols, the youth offered me a chair.

"How are you getting on with the school?"

"Pretty well, thank you. By the way, you can help me. Can you recommend a good person, a Komsomol, as leader of the Young Pioneers?"

"That is an important matter, and you must be very careful. The boys sometimes overreach themselves because of the great power they have over the non-party teachers."

"I know, but still I am obliged to have somebody. Can't you suggest someone?"

"I'm afraid not. We have a few Komsomols here whom I could trust, but the cell wouldn't let them go, and you wouldn't care for the worthless ones. They would only hurt your school."

"Couldn't you come yourself?"

"I'd like to, but the party wants me here. I'd love to get away from the city, though, and be among children. I am a peasant. My parents live in Tver province and I was raised on a farm."

I liked the boy. He seemed to have a free, independent mind, and he spoke with unusual frankness. His face was good-natured and honest, and there was a funny tuft of hair on the top of his head which did not seem in keeping with his high forehead and the serious expression of his blue eyes.

My visits to the Commissariat of Education were rather frequent. Once I found the secretary speaking to a shabbily dressed woman in the corridor. She had two small children with her and was crying.

"Will you step in?" the boy said to me. "I'll be back in a moment."

He was excited when he returned. "This damned bureaucracy!" he exclaimed. "And they call it the rule of the proletariat! Nothing is done for the people. They are left in their misery and poverty. They come here for help and wait for hours—and for what? Meetings, conferences, receptions. What's the use? We've done away with the bourgeoisie and given birth to a new bourgeoisie and a bureaucracy!"

I could not believe my ears. Here in the Commissariat of Education, at the source of the Bolshevik propaganda, a member of the Komsomol was talking heresy to me, a non-Communist, a bourgeois! He might be arrested for it and punished severely, but he was indifferent to that.

"Selfishness and contempt for the poor and unhappy are all you find. The welfare and happiness of the people mean nothing. There is misery everywhere. The woman you saw in the corridor has been here a dozen times already, waiting for hours. She's a widow with six children, one of them an idiot. She can't work, can't leave them, and can't put them in an orphanage, because all the homes are full."

His blue eyes darkened, his cheeks flushed, and he brushed his papers away.

"I'd like to go away so as not to see, not to . . ."

The door of the acting commissar's study opened and a small dark man with wavy hair and an enormous portfolio bowed himself out.

The bell rang. The secretary straightened, stood motionless a moment and then, with an energetic shake of his head, as if he wanted to rid himself of his thoughts and emotions, entered the commissar's room.

He was back in a moment, at the telephone.

"Five-seven-four-two. Garage? The car for the Acting Commissar of Education. And hurry up."

I was shown into the study. "Please, only seven minutes for you. The commissar is going to a meeting."

I never had a real opportunity to talk to the boy again. People were always coming in and out, asking to see the commissar or bringing papers from different departments for signature. The secretary was very busy. Only once I happened to be alone in the room with him for a few moments.

"I'd like to speak to you sometime," the boy said.

"I'll be glad to have you," I answered. "Only not today; I am leaving for the country tonight. But I shall be back in about a week."

On the way home, I thought of him and wished that I had talked with him longer. He had seemed depressed, and I knew by the expression of his eyes and his quivering voice that he had something important to tell me. I was never to know what it was.

Ten days later, when I called at the commissariat again, the door of his room was locked. People were moving about inside, shifting furniture, talking in low, excited tones. I stood at the door a moment and then knocked, but nobody answered. I asked a clerk in the next room what was the matter.

"The room is being cleaned. Call in about an hour."

As I was passing through the corridor, a girl whom I knew stopped me.

"Don't you know what's happened?"

"No."

"Comrade —— has committed suicide."

"What!"

"Yes. Five minutes ago. He shot himself in the temple. He was found at his desk, his head on his arm, all the papers spattered with blood . . . They are cleaning the room now . . ."

She chattered on, excited by her news. I did not hear. I was thinking of the serious boy with the sad blue eyes, the funny tuft of hair, and the big peasant hands.

"Why did he do it?"

"Oh, nobody knows," the girl answered, pleased at her chance to pursue this interesting subject. "The Communists say that although he was a good worker, he was a bad member of the party, not firm enough in his Communist faith, not really class conscious . . ."

THE governor's son was not accustomed to ask favors. It was hard for him. He lowered his eyes so that I could see only his long dark lashes, and his proud head drooped.

"They say I was excluded because I did not declare that my father was a governor. Why should I? They never asked me. I would have told them the truth if they had." And the boy looked into my face. "Do you think there is any hope? Will they let me graduate?"

He had a gentle voice, his manners and speech were refined; he rolled his r's a little as some members of the Russian aristocracy are apt to do. He never said "comrade" or spoke of the Communists by name, but always said "they," with distaste.

"The professors say that if I graduate, I could be of some use to them in the future. This is my last year, my work . . ."

He stopped short, and the blood rushed to his thin neck and face.

". . . You understand why I am telling you all this. It may help, when you ask them to let me go on in the university . . ."

I was sorry for the lad and willing to help him. I went from one official to another, and entreated them, but to no avail.

"Comrade," I would plead, "please make an exception for this boy. The professors say that he is very talented and will undoubtedly become a great chemist; his work . . ."

"Impossible, comrade! He is the son of a governor, our class enemy. He has deceitfully hidden his birth from us. We cannot allow people of his type to take advantage of the proletariat."

Everywhere I got the same answer. The boy went with me to the Commissariat of Education and waited for me in the corridor. He stood out from the crowd, looking very distinguished in his old but neat suit, carrying his handsome head high. And he attracted attention; people turned to look at him. I noticed a few girls staring at him with admiration; but there was hatred in the eyes of others.

"Refused?"

"Yes."

"Hopeless?"

"I don't know. I'll try to see the commissar; maybe . . ."

"Thank you. You know, I am still attending classes at the university. If they will admit me, I shan't have lost any time. Don't you think that's a good idea? Oh, I forgot to tell you: my parents are so grateful . . . They are sending you . . ."

"How are they?"

"Well, my father cannot walk; his feet are no better. But mother is all right, thank you. She was rather upset yesterday —they took us off the food cards because we're bourgeois, and we have some difficulty getting food now. You know how expensive it is in the market, and how hard to get. And they threaten to turn us out of our lodgings. But everything will be all right if I graduate from the university!"

Three weeks passed before I could get an appointment with the Commissar of Education. The boy came to me several times to ask how things were progressing. He seemed thinner and paler, and very weary.

My conversation with the commissar was brief. When I started to explain, he interrupted me brusquely:

"What are you wasting your time for? The boy cannot be admitted. Don't you think it would be rather foolish of us to destroy our enemies on the one hand, and give them a chance to study and hold positions that we want for the workers on the other?"

"But this is quite an unusual case," I argued. "The boy is a wonder. He is one of the most talented students in the university. His scientific ability may be useful to the country. How can you let a man of his talent be thrown out of the university when you need so many experts for the achievement of the Five Year Plan?"

"You know the saying, 'Chips fly when wood is chopped.' And we have plenty of talent among the proletariat!"

The boy came to see me that evening.

"My professor told me," he said, "that if Gorki could speak for me . . ."

"I must tell you the truth," I said, feeling as if I were plunging into ice-cold water. "I have been to the commissar today. There is no hope."

I looked into the boy's face. There was despair in the dark eyes.

"None at all?"

"Not for the present, I don't think so."

"Oh, what shall . . ."

He gave a little choking cough, turned sharply, and ran out of the room.

L

MENZHINSKY OF THE G.P.U.

WHENEVER I was in Moscow, my telephone rang from morning till night: a professor had been arrested or a friend of my father's was to be exiled to the north; one of the museum directors had been sent to prison; a monastery was going to be dissolved; some member of the old aristocracy was condemned to death; a clergyman was being prosecuted because of his influence on his parish, or the old church where Pushkin was married was to be torn down and some museum workers begged me to forward a petition to the Central Executive Committee, asking them to spare it. In each case it was hoped that my father's name would help.

There was an endless stream of such requests. Time had to be found for them between such duties as going to meetings, looking for teachers, buying textbooks, and asking the Department of Education for money with which to repair buildings, put up a schoolhouse, and pay the teachers. I even had to hunt all over Moscow for a secondhand microscope for the school; there was none to be bought in the stores. I was perpetually hurrying from one place to another, hanging to a strap in a crowded street car and hugging an armload of books.

In the morning before starting I planned where to go first and where next, so as not to lose a moment. The petition about Pushkin's church had to be given to Smidovich, Kalinin's assistant. He was a university graduate and intelligent, and would understand the value of the church better than anyone else. Some petitions went to the fat good-natured secretary of the Soviet Congress, the Georgian Enukidze; cases of arrest and capital punishment were brought before the Vice-President of the G.P.U., Menzhinsky.

LUBIANKA 2. I have to stand in line to get a pass.
"Who are you? What do you want?"

"I want permission to see Menzhinsky."

"Wait."

Telephone calls, questions, scrutiny. A wait of half an hour or an hour. At last the pass is shoved through the window. I show it to the secretary and wait again. The vice-president is busy. Finally the door opens, the heavy curtains part, and Menzhinsky asks me to come in. He is a Pole and he is courteous. He smiles, holds out his hand, and suddenly the blood rushes to my face.

"He takes me for one of his own people." I cannot bear the thought. I must make him understand at once that he is mistaken even if I ruin myself.

"When will the Soviet Government stop its abominable activity?" I ask.

"What do you mean?"

"Executing innocent people, putting them in prison, exiling them. There must be an end to these futile horrors."

The pleasant smile freezes, the friendliness in the eyes behind the glasses dies away, and they become sharp.

"We shall stop punishing people when the counterrevolutionary elements in our country are entirely destroyed!"

"Half of those whom you call counterrevolutionaries are dead already!" I say, and, getting back my self-possession, I begin talking about my friends. I speak intensely, putting all of myself into every word. Menzhinsky watches me like a hawk, trying to catch something that may be turned against those for whom I am pleading. He is a detective now. I know I must be truthful and sincere, and persuade him to trust every word I say. My friends are innocent, and, if I can make him believe me, I may win my case.

ONCE a writer came to me. I had known him when we worked together in the Zemstvo Union during the war. He came from Siberia where he had been a newspaper correspondent with Kolchak's army. He had had to spend years in hiding.

"I want to be legalized," he said. "Can you help me?"

"I don't know," I said doubtfully. "If you are ready to risk . . ."

"Yes, I am sick of this state of things. I can't write or do anything, and there's this eternal fear . . ."

Again I went to Menzhinsky.

"I am very tired today," he said. "I have been working all night long."

I imagined his work—I had a good idea of it from the number of friends and acquaintances of mine who had been arrested—and a shudder passed through me. He did not look like a gendarme—rather a typical intellectual, with a lock of hair falling over his forehead. But the look in his eyes was hard.

"I am going to speak to you candidly," I said, looking at him intently—"and you must believe every word I say."

"Hm . . ."

"I will give into your hands the life of a man who was your political enemy, who took part in the Kolchak movement."

"Where is he?" The eyes watched me.

"He is very far off. He is going under another name. But if you promise not to prosecute him, I will tell you all about him."

"Well, that could be done. But how do you expect me to promise? I know nothing about the man. Has he given up his counterrevolutionary activity? What is he doing now?" The eyes were piercing.

"I will tell you nothing until you promise not to harm him."

There was silence for a moment.

"Tell me one thing," Menzhinsky said. "Did he actually fight against us?"

"No."

"All right, I give you my word of honor as a Communist that I will not prosecute him, if he promises not to take part in counterrevolutionary work again."

And Menzhinsky kept his word. The man was legalized, and is living and writing in Moscow now.

LI

CHRIST IS A MYTH

ALL of us—children, teachers, museum workers, peasants—were living two lives, one the official, that is, the Bolshevik life, the other our own, which was being crushed and destroyed and driven far into the depths of our beings.

Even the youngest children were becoming hypocrites.

The old fluffy-haired inspector with the one yellow tooth came again. He examined the third grade in the primary school.

"Well, children, what have you got to show me?"

They brought out their writing and drawings and recited some poetry.

"Can you sing?"

The children looked at each other: "What shall we sing? The 'International'?"

When they finished he asked for some of their village folk songs, and they sang several.

"Tatiana Andreyevna," they asked when he had gone, "is the inspector a Communist?"

"No."

"He's not a Bolshevik?"

"Why, no, he isn't a member of the party."

"Oh! why didn't you tell us? Why did we sing the 'International' for him?"

There were many instances of our hypocritical living. One of the teachers was accustomed to speak against religion at meetings in the club house, but at night his wife would wake up and hear him singing hymns. Museum workers would refer to Tolstoy as a revolutionist who fought against the Orthodox church, and would avoid mentioning his religious ideas. The children burst out laughing when the Acting Commissar of Education, Comrade Epstein, asked if they went to church—and yet many of them were interested in religious questions.

Once, as I was passing through the corridor, I heard a number of voices talking loudly in the third grade. I went in.

"Oh, I'm so glad you've come!" the teacher said. "Please tell us what you think about God!"

"God?"

"Yes, yes!" one of the children shouted. "We want to know whether God exists or not."

"Of course He does, children!" I said, avoiding the alarmed glance of the teacher.

"I told you so!" a boy shouted. "I knew He did."

One of the Pioneers with a red necktie jumped up: "No, no, no! It's only the bourgeois who believe in God. And the priests who darken the poor people's minds and then rob them."

"My parents believe in God. They haven't thrown their ikons away . . ."

"Ikons, pieces of wood!" the Young Pioneer shouted.

"Who created the world, if there is no God?"

I stayed for almost an hour. The children wanted to know a great deal: Was it true that all priests were greedy? What did my father believe? Did I believe in a future life? I told them frankly what I thought.

"Please come and talk to us again—please!" one of the boys called as I left the room. The teacher followed me. "Well, what will happen now?" she asked.

I did not care. It was such a joy to be oneself. The excited childish voices were still ringing in my ears.

What is the use of trying to keep antireligious propaganda out of the school, I thought, and giving them nothing in its stead? What is the sense of forbidding "godless corners," with the posters of big-bellied, drunken clergymen, the figure of Christ embracing a bourgeois, and the ribald verse of Demian the Poor,[1] and not daring to tell the children about the teachings of Christ?

The Komsomols proposed to organize a society of "militant godless" at Yasnaia Poliana, and established "godless corners."

---

[1] A popular Soviet poet.

On Christmas Eve and the Saturday before Easter, the Komsomol, with the help of the local Communist cells, presented antireligious plays and movies and lectures. The older peasants were indignant; the girls and boys welcomed any kind of a show. Sometimes after the performance the Komsomols would go to the church where services were being held, and shout down the priest and sing ribald songs.

Some of the children had never heard the name of Christ. Others had got their ideas of him from the antireligious posters. Once, in a class in literature, the teacher asked the boys, "Where did Gogol go when he was traveling abroad?"

The children did not know.

"He went to Palestine. You know, of course, why Palestine is so famous?"

Silence.

At last one of the boys raised his hand.

"I know that one of those people who were called saints in the old days lived in Palestine; but what was his name? . . ."

The children were ignorant in religious and moral matters, and the teachers were afraid to instruct them. If a child happened to have an interest in such subjects, the teacher would either not answer his questions or would try to avoid giving a clear answer. Sometimes I thought of my father. I knew that he would have said: "It is better to let all those children be illiterate than to darken their minds as you are doing!"

And I was troubled.

EVERY Sunday hundreds of people came from Tula or from Moscow to visit Yasnaia Poliana. We could not show the museum to a group of more than twenty-five at a time, because many of the rooms were too small. Sometimes people were astonished to find that Tolstoy had lived so simply.

As soon as the visitors entered the hall Ilya Vasilievich would say, "Will you please take off your hats in honor of Lev Nikolayevich?" His quiet words always created an atmosphere of solemnity.

The most serious visitors were peasants, workers, and sol-

diers; the most inane—the so-called "Soviet girl employees."
Many of the workers, especially the middle-aged ones, had
read Tolstoy's books. Some of the Soviet employees had never
heard of him, and I did not know what to tell them. "He was
a poet, wasn't he?" they would ask. The young workers knew
nothing about Tolstoy's protests against the exploitation of the
poor, imprisonment, and capital punishment. His books were
only published in small editions in Russia now, and his
philosophical works were banned in the public libraries. The
teachers at Yasnaia even debated whether a complete set of
Tolstoy's works should be included when we were selecting the
books for the school library. I settled the matter by saying we
must have them and that there was to be no further discussion.

"Was your father against military service?" a Red army soldier asked me once.

"Yes."

"Why?"

While I was answering, a group of soldiers gathered. They
listened attentively and asked questions, neither laughing nor
arguing assertively. I felt a responsibility for what I said, not
because I was afraid the men would denounce me for my
"radical" ideas, but because they were so eager to know.

Once a group from the Communist school in Tula came to
see the museum. I dreaded their visit. This school was always
associated in my mind with disagreeable things: Cherniavsky
had been the director, and all the agitators and secretaries of
the Komsomol who were sent to us came from there.

I showed them the dining room first, and began telling them
about serfdom and my father's attitude toward it. When I
stopped and looked at the boys, I felt that I had their interest.

In the drawing room a copy of the *Thoughts of Wise Men,*
which my father had collected, was lying on the table. I told
them how he read this book every morning before he started
his day's work. "It was like a prayer to him," I said, and
stopped short, waiting for the word "prayer" to produce an
explosion. But the boys were still quiet.

"Let us read it, as he did," I said.

"Yes, please read it!"

I opened to a quotation from the Gospel.

"Who wrote those splendid words?" one of the boys asked.

"Christ said them."

"No! Christ couldn't have said that! Do you really believe that Christ existed? People prove to us nowadays that the story of Christ is nothing but a myth . . ."

I gave them some books: *The Teaching of Christ, Confession,* and a few others. We said cordial goodbyes.

Later in the afternoon I had to go to the school. As I passed through the park, I saw the students. They were all lying on the grass in a circle and reading aloud—the Bible!

LII

EXPLOITER AND EXPLOITED

"IT'S impossible, comrade!"

"What do you mean, 'impossible'? It will be as I say! Do you consider it just that you should occupy a room and your employee another, while a worker and his family are thrown out into the street?"

"But, if you take my room and put a family of five in it, our work can't go on. This is the office of the Tolstoy Society, which works on Tolstoy's manuscripts. The place must be quiet. With three children there will be noise and dirt, and what about our manuscripts? The place is so small!"

"You had better get rid of your bourgeois prejudices!" the President of the House Committee snapped. "The worker and his family can't stay out-of-doors, you have three rooms, and we are going to put them in here. That's all!"

"But there are three of us, a typist, the janitress and I, in two small rooms, and the big room is the office. Where will you put the family?"

"They can live in the bathroom or the kitchen, and, if you don't like it, give them your room," and the Communist went out, slamming the door.

After a week of waiting in the reception rooms of commissars, I succeeded in getting a document which protected me from this invasion of my apartment.

But a new difficulty awaited me.

Dunia, the janitress, was a kind, quiet girl. She had a child as the result of an unfortunate love affair. I was sorry for her and did her work myself while she was in the hospital. She sent the baby to an asylum, and came back to us.

One day I discovered that some jewelry that had been my mother's was missing. It was found in Dunia's room. She seemed to be very sorry, cried, and begged me to forgive her, which I willingly did; but I asked her to leave. She went to the

President of the House Committee. The same Communist
who had been concerned in the affair of the worker's family
took her part, and told her that as a member of the House Committee she had a right to live in my apartment. He also advised
her to go to her trade-union and ask for protection.

Dunia refused to leave. She stayed on and charged me with
making her work more than eight hours, which was against the
law. I advised her to withdraw her charge. She listened attentively and seemed almost persuaded. But after she had seen the
Communist again, she was obstinate, accused me of overwork-
ing and "exploiting" her, and catalogued her grievances at
length.

"Dunia, you know that is not true . . ." I said.

"Yes, it's true, it's true," she gasped, "all of you bourgeois are
like that, exploiting, tormenting us poor people . . . but now
it's our turn to have our way, and you don't dare . . ."

What was to be done? She had robbed me; she had brought
charges against me, yet there she was all day long in my apartment, and I could not turn her out! A lawyer told me that the
only way to get rid of her was to charge her with theft.

Several weeks passed. At last I was informed that the two
trials had been set for the same day: Dunia's suit against me
for overtime, which might result in my having to pay her several hundred rubles; and my charge against her for theft.

"Citizen Judges!" Dunia's lawyer exclaimed pathetically,
"who has not read Tolstoy's famous *Resurrection!* Who does
not know the name of Katiusha Maslova? Citizen Judges!
Katiusha Maslova is standing before you. Who is she? An im-
poverished worker, one of those who has been exploited all her
life by the rich. And, on the other side, you have before you a
representative of the old aristocracy, a bourgeois, a countess,
who inherited none of the simplicity and wisdom of her father!
And this aristocrat, this unworthy daughter of a great father,
wants to imprison this miserable, defenseless girl, one of the
oppressed."

Dunia was sobbing. I was sure that my case was lost, that I

should have to spend the rest of my life in the apartment with Dunia.

I had no lawyer. I spoke for myself.

"Citizen Judges!" I said. "Allow me to point out to you a small mistake that the citizen lawyer made in his brilliant speech. Yes, this woman would certainly have been one of the defenseless and oppressed in the time of the Tsar. I should never have charged her with theft in the old days, because she would undoubtedly have been punished and put in prison. If I charge her with theft now, it is because I know that the court will be merciful to a proletarian, a poor lost woman, and will not imprison her."

I won the case. Dunia was not convicted but she had to leave the apartment.

LIII

COMRADE STALIN

IT occurred to me that celebrating the hundredth anniversary of Tolstoy's birth would emphasize the work we were doing in his name and might keep the local Communists quiet for a while. And I thought that by inviting the Soviet authorities and foreign visitors and declaring my "credo" in their presence, I might safeguard the schools and museum of Yasnaia Poliana. I was ingenuous enough to believe that we could continue existing as an oasis in the middle of a desert.

We began to make plans and estimates in 1926 for a Jubilee to be held on August 28, 1928. The plans were ambitious, and included the following:

1. The publication of Tolstoy's complete works in about ninety volumes, to be edited by the Tolstoy Society and Chertkov. To include diaries, letters, variants, unpublished works, and articles formerly prohibited by the tsarist censor.

2. The reorganization of the Tolstoy Museum in Moscow and its removal to a stone house.[1] The construction of a new library for manuscripts; the rebuilding of Tolstoy's house in Khamovnichesky Street; supplementing of collections, and so on.

3. The repair of all the museum buildings at Yasnaia Poliana; the construction of roads through the estate; the cataloguing of the library; the organization of a new museum in the annex to portray "Tolstoy at Yasnaia Poliana"; a new library containing books about Tolstoy; and so on.

4. The building of a hospital with thirty beds, with a surgical department, a child clinic, and nurseries.

5. The construction of the school in memory of Tolstoy. New kindergartens, workshops, a home for teachers, etc.

---

[1] This was never done. The museum with its fine collection of photographs, portraits, books, and other objects is still where it was.

A Jubilee Committee was appointed by the government. The chairman was the Commissar of Education, Lunacharsky; the members: Chertkov, Gusev, a delegate from the Yasnaia Poliana peasants, the President of the Tula Provincial Executive Committee, a few professors—the editors of Tolstoy's works—and myself.

All the plans and estimates had to be worked out and passed by the Jubilee Committee, and approved by the government. We estimated that we would need a million rubles.

In 1926 a small sum of money had been given by the government for constructing the school. Instead of buying bricks for the walls, I bought a forest in Kaluga district, and spent the summers of 1926 and 1927 organizing brick production. About two million bricks were made, a million for the school and a million for the hospital. When I sent my accounts to the Department of Education, they reprimanded me. Why was I buying forests and building brick kilns? I proved that with bricks selling at sixty-five to seventy rubles a thousand instead of ten rubles a thousand, as before the Revolution, it was cheaper to make them. Besides I could not have got enough from the Tula factories; they were all taken by the government.

The walls were built, and the woodwork, doors, and furniture were made in our workshops by the boys and teachers. But there was no money for the roof, floors, or heating system. And there were no funds for the museum. Less than a year was left and very little had been done. I decided to go to Stalin himself and ask whether the government intended to carry through the celebration or not. After several months spent in vain trips to Moscow, I succeeded in getting an audience.

As I entered the big house in a byway near the Old Chinese wall, a soldier standing by the entrance stopped me.

"Excuse me, comrade, I must look at your portfolio."

He peeped between the papers, gave it back, and while he opened the elevator door for me, kept on studying me.

Another soldier met me upstairs.

"Comrade Stalin? This way!"

The reception room was not large. A clerk was sitting at a desk. From here, through a corridor, one might go to any of the three secretaries: Stalin, Kaganovich, or Smirnov.

"You will have to wait. Comrade Stalin is busy."

I sat down and looked about. People were coming and going. Most of them wanted to see Kaganovich. The doors opened so quietly that I did not hear the secretary come into the room.

"Comrade Stalin is waiting for you."

I was shown into a large room with a desk at the other end. A very tall man rose to meet me. "Georgian politeness," I thought.

"Sit down, please!" he said with a marked Caucasian accent.

I tried to make my speech as short and clear as possible.

"Your estimates are too high," he said. "We are poor and cannot afford to give you such a sum of money just now. What is the minimum you need for the celebration of the Jubilee?"

I did some quick reckoning.

"All right, I will try and do what I can."

"And how about the publication of Tolstoy's works? The Gosizdat has not yet decided to publish and the government has not granted any money for the publication. Perhaps you do not want Tolstoy's books published because of his religious views . . ."

"We admire Tolstoy as a writer," Stalin said. "We are not afraid of his influence on the masses."

Stalin reminded me outwardly of a noncommissioned officer in the Tsar's guard, or a gendarme, with his thick mustache, regular but coarse features, narrow forehead and stubborn, vigorous chin. He was too polite for a Bolshevik. As I was leaving, he rose again and escorted me to the door.

LIV

THE JUBILEE

IT rained for several days before the Jubilee. Sinking to their knees in mud, the men tore down the brick kilns and finished the roads. The last exhibits of "Tolstoy at Yasnaia Poliana," were being hung in the new museum. In the assembly hall "The Power of Darkness" and some of my father's stories, made into plays, were being rehearsed. Some of the children were busy making programs. Korolev's bust of Tolstoy stood in a niche at the entrance to the school.

A few days before the Jubilee, the President of the Tula Executive Committee sent for me. How were we going to transport our guests from the station? Could we serve luncheon in a brick shed? What would we do for interpreters? It was easy to reassure him on this last question: eight European languages were spoken in our group.

On the day of the Jubilee I went to the station to meet the guests at 7 A.M. It was pouring. The station was full of busses and automobiles sent by the Tula Provincial Executive Committee. A crowd of curious people, a few local Communists, and delegates from the Yasnaia Poliana peasants were waiting on the platform.

The special car with the guests stopped in front of the station, and the solid figure of Lunacharsky, the Commissar of Education, appeared, surrounded by a crowd. I noticed at once the pleasant smiling face of Chekhova-Knipper—the wife of Anton Chekhov—and the picturesque head of Professor Sakulin with his curly hair and wide-brimmed hat. The foreigners could be distinguished by their good clothes and shoes, and the cameras slung over their shoulders. They had an expectant look, as if prepared to see this wild country produce strange things. Newspaper men moved quickly through the crowd, pursuing celebrities.

The official meeting took place in the morning. It was long, tedious, and melancholy. Comrade Stepanov, the President of the Tula Provincial Executive Committee, made the first speech. He talked for twenty minutes in a vicious circle, and at the end could not conclude. The longer he spoke, the more entangled he became, until at last, with his face purple, and drops of perspiration glistening on his forehead, he tied himself in an inextricable knot and stopped. The simple, hearty speech of our student Vitia Goncharov was very welcome after this. The dean, looking frequently at her notes, gave a smooth but rather tedious account of our school work. I was obliged to improvise, and spoke badly. Through all this Lunacharsky smiled and chatted with his neighbors. Suddenly he squeezed my hand and said, "I am very fond of you, Alexandra Lvovna!" This was so funny and so unexpected that I could not help laughing.

Veleminsky, who had known my father, spoke for the foreign guests in a mixture of Russian and Slovenian which no one could understand very well. He concluded by saying that all the foreign guests begged the Soviet Government to allow the daughter of Tolstoy to continue her work in the schools and museum in accord with the ideas of Tolstoy. Here his voice failed him, his eyes got red, and he could not continue. I was very much touched. His emotion was obviously genuine.

"Anatole Vasilievich!" I said to Lunacharsky, feeling that the moment had come to declare my creed. "Allow me to answer."

"What are you going to say?"

"I want to describe the exceptional position of Yasnaia Poliana—how the Soviet Government . . ."

"Alexandra Lvovna Tolstoy will speak."

Like a drowning man, I grasped at this last opportunity to make secure the status of Yasnaia Poliana.

". . . the Soviet Government so respects the name of Tolstoy, that while militarism and antireligious propaganda are taught in all the schools of Russia, Yasnaia Poliana is privileged, in honor of Tolstoy, to avoid those questions."

As soon as I had finished speaking, Lunacharsky got up, and

in a sonorous voice, with the poise of an experienced speaker, delivered a typical Red oration. "We are not afraid," he said, "that the students of the Yasnaia Poliana school will be educated in a Tolstoyan spirit foreign to our aims. We are deeply persuaded that when the youngsters of this school enter our colleges and universities, we shall be able to mold them in our own way. We shall purge them of all Tolstoyanism and make them into strong fighting troops that will support our socialist government."

It was the usual Communist harangue, but it was a catastrophe for the Tolstoyan organizations.

Very pleased with himself, Lunacharsky, followed by the whole crowd, made his way toward the hall, where the guests stood in a half circle on the two wings of the staircase in front of the niche and waited for the official opening of the new school. Here the Commissar of Education delivered another speech. This time he spoke of Tolstoy's influence upon his own boyhood. There was feeling in his words and a tremor in his voice, and when he finished, with a quick theatrical gesture he tore the canvas from Korolev's bust of my father. The ceremony was over, and my hopes with it.

The foreigners were tired and hungry. For several hours they had listened to speeches they could not understand. Stefan Zweig came to tell me that he had always admired my father; the Swedish delegate tried to talk to me in English; Veleminsky told of his former visit to Yasnaia Poliana. One of the foreigners discovered that his camera had disappeared and someone tried to prove that it had been stolen by one of the newspaper men.

A cold and tasteless lunch was served in one of the brick sheds, and afterward we showed the guests the estate and house. We had to give explanations in several languages, which was hard, since many of us had had no opportunity of speaking French or English for years.

The rain had stopped, but the day was still gray when we went to father's grave. The guests took their hats off and approached the evergreen hedge in silence.

"No monument, no flowers even," someone said.

"He liked the oak trees better than monuments. We tried to plant flowers, but it is too shady, they don't grow."

Veleminsky and a few others knelt. Professor Sakulin delivered a short speech, and we all went back.

The teachers invited the foreign guests to their homes. "You can rest and have a cup of tea."

They refused. One man was on the point of accepting but suddenly he asked:

"And where is Lunacharsky? No, no, thank you. I am afraid he will be displeased."

We got the impression that the foreign visitors were afraid of something. It seemed strange, for we thought of foreigners as free.

In the evening the children's chorus sang music of Beethoven, Tchaikovsky, and Rimsky-Korsakov. Vitia read a composition, "The Yasnaia Poliana Peasants' Reminiscences of Tolstoy," which he and another boy had written with the help of their teacher. It was a good job and Vitia read well. He stood in the middle of the platform, ruffled his curly black hair, and enjoyed the laughter of the audience.

The last number on the program was the greatest success. The curtain was drawn to reveal some twenty peasant women standing in a circle on the stage, all dressed in old-fashioned, local costumes—white blouses with embroidered sleeves, gold trimmed petticoats, and red, yellow, and green dresses. These costumes had not been worn in the villages for thirty or forty years. We had hunted for them everywhere, dragging them from the bottom of the women's trunks. The best singers and dancers in the village had been invited. An old peasant, Spiridonych, in a glowing red shirt, wide trousers, and high boots greased with tar, and Grandma Avdotia from Kaznacheyevka acted out the songs with gestures. The old sad songs were followed by gay dance and wedding tunes. When, during the last song, Vaska Vorobiev darted out of the circle and danced with his sister, the whole audience, including the commissar and the foreign guests, jumped up and applauded wildly.

Meanwhile, downstairs in the teacher's room, correspondents

were telephoning to the Moscow papers, although some of them had sent their reports before the meeting began. The next morning we had a surprise: There was not a word of praise for Yasnaia Poliana in any of the Soviet newspapers. *Pravda* criticized the government for neglecting to supervise more carefully a school where half-starved children were forced to sing hymns. Beethoven had sounded like the Christian menace to someone's unaccustomed ears.

LV

EXCURSIONS

H ERE they are! In the snow just like two wine bottles! Get up! One, two, three, four, five, six! That's right— six!"

The stout teacher and I struggled to our feet, shaking the snow out of our sleeves and necks and felt boots. Everybody was laughing.

In the village we had just left our Lapland driver had had several drinks. Perhaps that was why his thoughts ran on bottles. He drove the first sleigh, and the two other teams of reindeer were tied behind it, one after the other. It was four o'clock in the afternoon, but absolutely dark. We could hardly make out the fantastic branching of the reindeer's horns. Sometimes we dove suddenly down hill. The Laplander was much too drunk to put on the brakes, and the animals, trying to get away from the sleigh which was hitting their hind legs, flew over the snow. The little sleighs were smooth, like Finnish toboggans, and it was very difficult to keep from falling off.

Once in a while the Laplander would stop.

"What's the matter?"

"One, two, three, four . . ."

He did not want to lose any of us, for he was to get six rubles from each one for the drive.

We were a party of teachers and museum workers on an excursion organized by the Commissariat of Education at Christmas, 1928. We spent four days in Murmansk, the new Soviet port of the Far North, the "gateway to the Arctic Ocean," and the only city in Russia that had no churches. The whole party —both men and women—was lodged in one room, which was dirty, infested with bugs, and devoid of beds. We had to sleep on the bare floor.

It was very cold—50° below zero. The sun was invisible and it was half dark all day long. We loitered about the market. A young woman in a white "malitsa"[1] embroidered at the bottom and white deerskin shoes drove up in a sleigh covered with reindeer skins.

"That's Uliana," a local teacher told us. "She is well known here. She's a widow and does men's work, and no one can drive reindeer the way she can. She's a clever one. Last year when the Soviets requisitioned deer, she hid hers in the woods so they couldn't be found. Nobody knows how many she's got."

We wanted to buy fur for shubas. In the center of town we found a small government store, but it had in stock only a few fur mittens and shoes.

"We send all the fur abroad," the salesman told us.

We tried to buy some deerskins from the Laplanders.

"No, no, we haven't any," they kept saying. "We have given all the skins to the government."

The teacher told us that the year before thousands of deer had been requisitioned from the Laplanders and slaughtered. Most of the skins could not be used because the animals were killed at a time when the fur was poor. After that the Laplanders hid their animals in the woods and swamps.

The old port of Alexandrovsk, situated near the open ocean, was abandoned now. An icebreaker that was being sent to the rescue of two boats which were icebound near Alexandrovsk took us there. We found a few deserted houses, a small biological station, and in it a scientist with his collections. "How can he live here alone in semidarkness, among bare rocky mountains, beside this cold ocean?" I wondered.

On our way back we stopped at Kandalaksha, a small town near the shore of the White Sea. It used to be one of the places that supplied all Russia with salmon and herring. Now only one factory was left.

"Last year we had enormous quantities of fish," the manager told us. "We didn't know what to do with them. About 800,-000 pounds of herring spoiled."

"Oh, why?" I asked, thinking of the food lines in Moscow.

---

[1] A deerskin garment with the fur inside, made like a wide shirt, with fur cap and mittens attached.

"We hadn't enough barrels to salt them in, and no tins. I really don't know what the people in Moscow are thinking about."

Loaded with smoked and salted fish, we started home. We had a five-day journey ahead of us before we got to Petersburg. At one of the first stations our train stopped for a while. I walked along the platform. A group of ragged men—one of them a priest—followed by soldiers passed me.

"Keep out of the way!" one of the soldiers shouted. "Can't you see we're guarding prisoners?"

In July, 1929, I was in Yaroslavl, one of the most ancient cities of northwest Russia. I wanted to visit a monastery that was built in the thirteenth century.

"You won't see much of it," a woman whom I asked about it told me. "They've turned it into a factory for felt boots."

I could hardly recognize the monastery. The walls lay in ruins, and there was a pile of stones in the middle of the yard. One of the chapels was being demolished.

"What do you want here?" a man asked me.

"I wanted to see the monastery."

"Well, you won't see it. They started a factory, but it didn't work. Now they want to use the stone for something."

"Let me carry your things for you."

"Oh, no, Father, thank you. This is too heavy."

An old priest, followed by a woman who was carrying his bag, was getting on the same boat. As it shoved off we stood on the deck watching Yaroslavl diminish in the distance. Its dirt and dust and ruins disappeared, and the calm beauty of the river spread in front of us.

"I'm on my way home from Moscow," the old clergyman said. "What do you think of their destroying the Iberian Chapel?"[2]

[2] The Chapel of the Iberian Virgin, built in 1669, was one of the most highly revered in prerevolutionary Russia. It attracted thousands of pilgrims from all parts of Russia and was usually crowded even at night. When the Tsar came to Moscow he always visited it before entering the Kremlin.

"I was in Moscow the day they tore it down," I answered. "I saw it one evening; the next morning when a friend and I were passing through Voskresenskaya Square on a street car, it was gone!"

"And the people?"

"They did not dare say anything. I opened my mouth, but I said nothing. We were afraid to speak, we only looked at each other."

The old man sighed. "To think that the Iberian Chapel . . ."

THE Volga was getting wider.

"Come and visit me," the old man said. "I live alone, alone with God."

"How do you get along, Father?"

"They take care of me—my friends, the peasants of our village. They give me more than I need. Oh, they are splendid people. You will see them, they will meet me."

SUNSET. We are still on deck. I cannot tear my eyes from the river. With much splashing and gurgling the ship is backing toward a small wharf.

"There is my home near the church."

Yes, I see the little white church with the gold dome half hidden among the trees. And there is a boat rowing toward the ship. The men are waving their hats, the women their handkerchiefs. The clergyman has taken off his shabby hat; he is smiling. Why are my eyes full of tears?

FOR two days we had no bread on the ship and we could not get any in the ports.

"Never mind," the passengers said, "as soon as we get to Tsaritsyn, the granary of Russia, you know, we'll be able to buy plenty from the peasants."

But when the steamboat stopped at the big city and we hurried to get off, a crowd of ragged peasants surrounded us.

"Bread! Bread!" they pleaded. "Give us some bread! We haven't eaten for days."

I STOPPED at Nizhni Novgorod to see the fair. Where in the old days there had been goods stacked high, now there were empty stalls. At last I found a booth of peasant handicraft. They made a poor display. The manager was very polite. He knew that I was the daughter of Leo Tolstoy and he was eager to show me all he had.

"We have been very successful with furs," he told me. "We make all kinds of furs out of cats, dogs, and rabbits. Don't these lapins look like sables?"

"Well, I don't know . . . Where are all the furs we used to get?"

"Oh, I guess they export them. But don't you think these look nice?"

He showed me a stall where only foreigners were admitted. It contained the work of the peasant artists who once painted ikons; now they did lacquer boxes and dishes. It was strange to see faces of saints in beautiful gold robes and to read the inscription, "The Soviet Meeting."

The manager told me that the work of these peasants had been nationalized, that they were not allowed to sell anything privately, and that the government bought all they produced and paid very little for it.

"Can't I buy something?" I asked.

"Oh, no," the man answered. "These things are not for us. Only foreigners—rich Americans—can buy them with foreign currency. But not Russians!"

LVI

THE ELECTION

THERE was one question that the peasants never failed to ask when they came to the estate. First they would look around to make sure that no one could hear them; then they would say, "What do you think, Alexandra Lvovna, will it soon be over?"

They asked it just as they would ask about something that was sent from above—a drought or a snowstorm.

"We can't bear it any longer. Now they've started those collective farms. Join the collective, you'll be ruined; don't join it, you'll be ruined. They're giving the best land to the collectives —the good fields, woods, credits, everything. But nothing will come of it. Who were the first to join? All the riffraff: Ivan the Ram, a drunkard; Boriska, the lame one, a drunkard and a loafer. Well, Tit Ivanovich had to, or they would have called him a kulak . . . Now he's worried. He's got a two-story brick house. How can he move it to the collective land? And take me, for example. What shall I do? I don't want to go to a collective farm and I am afraid not to. When will we be rid of this damned Bolshevism?"

"Nobody knows . . ."

"Sometimes we think our only salvation is war."

"War?"

"Yes. If we have a war, the guns will be in our hands. You don't really believe that we are going to kill Japs or Germans? No, thanks . . . The Kremlin is our worst enemy!"

ONCE two peasants came to talk to me.

"We want to elect our own man as president of the coöperative."

"Who?"

"Peter Ivanovich."

"He's a good man. I'll be glad to vote for him."

"It isn't an easy job, though. The members of the party want their own candidate."

"Let's try."

When I went to the club, it was full, and there was an angry crowd outside, blocking the door.

"What's the matter?"

"The Komsomol cell and the old administration have promised bread and sausage to those who will vote their way."

With difficulty I made my way to a front row. The crowd quieted down and the meeting went on smoothly until the peasants noticed that some of the students, Komsomols who were not of age, were taking part in the election. We protested, but the Komsomols and Communists clamored so that we gave up arguing. It was evident that the majority was still on our side.

When the hands[1] were counted, they made a mistake in their own favor which we hastened to protest. Finally Peter Ivanovich was elected president and I was made vice-president of the coöperative.

The next day the new administration had its first meeting. We made plans for buying goods in Moscow instead of Tula, in order to provide all the members of the coöperative with everything they needed at lower prices and avoid bread lines. Our plans were not realized. Three days later we were notified by the Central Tula Coöperative that the election was not valid: students who were not of age had been allowed to vote. There would have to be a new election.

"The crooks!" the peasants said. "They make the youngsters vote and then they turn it against us."

"Let's try again," I urged.

"No, I think I'd better refuse to run," Peter Ivanovich said, "they won't let me work anyhow. And they'll probable prosecute me . . ."

But we persuaded him to try once more.

There was less of a crowd this time. The first two rows on

---

[1] The Soviet Government has no secret ballot.

the left were filled with girls none of us knew. They were cracking sunflower seeds and giggling.

"Where do they come from?" I asked Peter Ivanovich. "They're not from our village."

"No, they're from Kaznacheyevka. The secretary of the Komsomol cell admitted thirty girls into the coöperative yesterday. He gave each of them a receipt for the fifty kopeks entrance fee so that they could vote for the member of the party."

The front rows on the right were filled with people dressed mostly in leather coats, with portfolios in their laps. There were several boys from the Communist school in Tula, and the local authorities: the president of the local executive committee, the secretary of the Communist party, and others. Although not members of our coöperative, they took part in the discussions and voted.

"They've got all the members of the party here," the peasants whispered, "there's no use trying, we've lost!"

We had certainly lost. The Communist machinery worked very efficiently and their candidate was quickly elected.

I carried my indignation to the secretary of the party in Tula. I told him all about the election: about the students, how the peasants were bought with sausage and bread, how the Komsomol had miscounted the votes. . . . He interrupted me:

"Well, what of it? What do you want? Haven't they elected a Communist?"

"Yes, but the election was illegal."

"What of that? It only proves how smart our people are! As for those tricks of theirs—you can't do without them. The end justifies the means."

The peasants refused to go to any more coöperative meetings.

"Why should we? What's the use? For twelve years we've been playing the comedy: electing representatives to soviets, voting for the managers of coöperatives. We're sick of it . . . If they want a president for the agricultural coöperative, they can have the Communist in the checked cap who has been lounging about the village. Only why should we elect him when he's appointed by the government?"

The bell rang—the signal for a meeting. No one went. At last about twenty Komsomols gathered in the club house and the Communist in the checked cap was elected.

The form was preserved but the essence of the free vote was killed. The coöperatives degenerated into government depots, providing the population with beggarly shares of goods.

LVII

A "MODEL TRIAL"

THE persecution of the kulak started in 1928. Many of them were ruined and exiled. Tit Ivanovich was the only peasant at Yasnaia Poliana who had a two-story brick house and who could be called a kulak. He had been an estate manager. With the Revolution, he became a turncoat. Once he had been devoted to the landowning class; now he supported the Bolsheviks. He was what our peasants called "a belly Communist," or a radish, "Red outside, White inside." Tit Ivanovich's eldest son was an agent of the Moscow G.P.U.; all his other children were Komsomols.

The Communists succeeded in finding other kulaks in our village: a man who had once been a policeman in Tula, another who had owned a small lumber yard, anyone who opposed the collectivization of the farms or who would not sow more grain than he needed for himself. The government was forcing the peasants to join the collective farms, hoping that those farms would produce enough grain to export. The peasants, understanding very well the government policy, would not till the soil beyond their own needs and sold many of their horses and cattle.

"What is the use of sweating and bending our backs?" they said. "We sow and the government reaps."

Goods became scarce on the market. The coöperative food cards provided us with one tenth of the food we needed. We could get black bread every day, but it was half baked and so heavy that we could not eat it. We had to buy eggs, butter, flour, cereal, and sugar at the market. Those who received high wages, two or three hundred rubles a month, could afford them; but teachers and workers who got only fifty rubles were always hungry. In 1929 the employees at Yasnaia Poliana had to pay 1.25 rubles a pound for flour at the Tula private market. But the government at that time was buying flour for export from the peasants on the Volga for three kopecks a pound. My wages were now four hundred and fifty rubles a month, but they were not sufficient to buy clothes and shoes. What could peasants who were selling their goods at the low government prices buy for their money?

THE news spreads in the village: "Tomorrow the coöperative will give madapollam."[1] The peasants never say "the Coöperative will sell"; the coöperative only "gives"—you don't choose what you want, you take what you get.

All the women rush to the coöperative. There is a line at one or two o'clock in the morning. The first ten to fifteen women get all there is in the shop, two or three yards each. The Communists and the Komsomols have already been supplied.

Someone reports, "Sugar is being sold in Tula, and very cheap, too." Employees from the museum and school and peasants hasten to the city. Big loaves of sugar are sold for one ruble twenty-five a kilogram. It is a strange kind of loaf sugar; it does not break, but crumbles into powder.

"It's good sugar, anyhow," one of the clerks says. "It was exported, but wasn't accepted; it was too soft. That is why you are getting it for such a low price!"

"They're giving out frozen zanders in Tula!" a peasant tells me. "Cheap—ten kopeks a pound. I got some yesterday. Maybe you won't like them. They smell a bit; but I don't mind, we haven't eaten fish for so long."

I did not buy any. They were so spoiled that the smell stayed with one for hours. They, too, had traveled abroad.

Sheep, pigs, cows were slaughtered, both by individual and collective farmers. Those who stayed on their own farms killed their live stock because they wanted money and food, and because the animals might be taken away from them. Those who joined collectives did not consider the farms their own and slaughtered the cattle at random.

The government passed laws, printed circulars, and sent Communists and Komsomols into the villages to urge peasants

[1] A kind of cotton cloth.

to till the soil. People were exiled or put in prison for "sabotaging" the crops. The administration of the Yasnaia Poliana agricultural and banking coöperative was brought to trial for this.

The president of the coöperative was the head doctor of our hospital—a scholar, botanist, member of the first Duma, and one of those who signed the Viborg Appeal[2] and were deprived of nobility by the Tsar's government. He was busy with the dispensary, distant visits, and the organization and building of the hospital; he could devote but little time to the work of the coöperative. The other two members of the coöperative were honest and energetic but uneducated young peasants. They misunderstood a paragraph in their circular of instructions directing that grain be given gratis to the poor peasants, the *"bedniaks,"* and they charged several of them for oats. Their other crime was not at once giving credit to a widow who wanted to buy a cow.

A "model" trial was held in the club house of Yasnaia Poliana. Nearly all the peasants were present, as well as the teachers and employees of the schools and museums. The presiding judge, a big red-haired man of peasant type, was sent from Tula; the other two judges were from our Chekino district. A Communist, the director of the Chekino district school, acted as prosecutor. All the witnesses on the side of the accused were challenged by the presiding judge, and only the witnesses against them remained.

The doctor was accused of being a malicious damager, of frustrating the campaign for sowing grain at the very time when the government was trying to destroy the kulaks and counterrevolutionary elements in the villages and to persuade the peasants to join collectives so that they might have plenty of grain both for their own needs and for building up the socialist government. He must be punished unmercifully; he was

---

[2] After the dissolution of the First Duma by Nicholas II (1906), its members gathered in Viborg, Finland, and issued an appeal to the Russian nation to resist the government by refusing to pay taxes and to do military service. The appeal had no marked results, but those who signed it were tried and lost their franchise.

one of those landowners and nobles who, profiting by the people's darkness, were trying to sneak into the Soviet institutions and destroy them. As for the other two members of the administration, they had the typical kulak psychology and they were frustrating the entire Soviet policy in the village.

One of the witnesses asserted that the doctor paid no attention to government circulars, but stuffed them into his portfolio instead of forwarding them to the agent of the Department of Agriculture.

"I can prove this," the agent said. "I saw such a paper lying on the table of the president of the coöperative and he never showed it to me, as he is supposed to do."

"May I ask you to describe the circular you speak of?" the doctor inquired.

"It was a small piece of paper, folded in four . . ."

"Perhaps this?" and he took a paper out of his portfolio.

"Yes, yes, that is it!"

"Will you please read it aloud?" the doctor said, handing the paper to the presiding judge.

"Well, that isn't necessary . . ."

"Oh, yes, it is! This paper is an order from a peasant for oats. I have never concealed circulars from the local authorities."

"We'll see about that later," the presiding judge muttered, and the paper disappeared into his folder.

The widow who had not received credit in time to buy her cow was called.

"What can you tell us about the matter?" the presiding judge asked.

"Oh, what can a poor illiterate woman like me say?" she moaned. "They are doing it all on purpose, trying to cheat a poor woman. All the kulaks get credit in time, while I . . ."

There was a recess in the middle of the trial. I went outside for a breath of fresh air.

"Alexandra Lvovna! Alexandra Lvovna! We want to speak to you." A group of peasants followed me out of the club.

"What have they done? What are they being tried for? We

couldn't have a better president than the doctor! Please speak
to the judges. Tell them!" they shouted, interrupting each
other.

"Friends!" I said, looking around nervously. "Don't hurt
both yourselves and me. Please go away! You don't know how
dangerous it is for us to be seen talking. The Communists will
say that we are planning a riot. Go and speak to the president
yourselves!"

They understood and turned away. I watched them with a
sad heart. I had known them from my childhood; many had
grown up, others had grown gray before my eyes. Now I did
not even dare to talk to them.

The presiding judge stood with a small group of Communists and smoked. The peasants approached him. I caught a
few words. "Very good man . . . We don't want a better president . . . He has done a lot for us . . ." Then a shrill young
voice said: "It's the Komsomol cell that is doing mischief here.
Take those secretaries away from Yasnaia Poliana. We don't
want them."

There was an uproar, and, as the presiding judge tried to
calm the peasants, another shrill voice drowned all the others:

"Comrades! It's Tolstaia who is stirring up the people!"

Again the peasants shouted, and the judge tried to quiet
them. Suddenly the secretary of the Komsomol cell darted out
of the crowd.

"I heard it all, comrades!" he shouted as he ran up the steps
of the club. "Tolstaia is setting the peasants against the Soviet
Government. Shall we never get rid of these bourgeois?"

"Do you know who the judges were?" a peasant asked me,
after these gentlemen had departed and it had been announced
that the trial would be continued in Tula. "I don't know about
the presiding judge—he's from Tula—but the other two are
from our district. The tall bony one who sat at the left was
tried himself for killing his wife a few years ago. And the other
one was tried once for violating a girl and a second time for
torturing prisoners. He was drunk, took them into the yard in

winter and pumped water over them. They nearly froze to death."

I went to Moscow to the Central Executive Committee to plead for the doctor and the two peasants. It may have helped. They were sentenced conditionally to three years in prison.

How true and how ironic was the speech of the doctor's lawyer:

"Citizen Judges! The doctor seems to be a person who never sings in tune. Under the Tsar he sang off pitch, and he was persecuted; he is not in tune now. He is like a singer with a chronic cold."

LVIII

I CAN LIE NO MORE

THE Jubilee did us no good. Yasnaia Poliana was swept along with the wave of Stalin's reorganization.

The nearest Communist cell was at Shchokino, about six miles away. In order to keep a closer watch over Yasnaia Poliana the Communists decided in 1928 to organize a cell there. At least three party members were required for starting one. Up to that time there had not been a single Communist among the peasants of Yasnaia Poliana, but now a dull illiterate girl was rapidly promoted from the Komsomol into the party. She became the representative of our farm workers in the trade-union of the estate, and later was elected one of the administrators of the coöperative.

The second Communist was sent from Tula and given the job of postman. The third, Trofimov, who also came from Tula, was made secretary of the cell. He had no other employment. He was a young worker with a broad freckled face, a deeply wrinkled forehead, and gray eyes which never looked directly at you. He was the instigator of the antireligious propaganda and military training in the club house, and he acted as if he had the right to meddle with all our institutions. His assumption that he could talk to the children or call meetings without asking permission annoyed me. But what shocked me most was his marching into my father's rooms, cap on head, with the air of master.

Gradually all the high positions in the coöperative and in the club house were occupied by Communists. Veshnev, a writer, was appointed assistant director of the Tolstoy museums.

"I think we can easily use Tolstoy's articles against the Orthodox church," he said to me, as if he had no doubt that I was of his opinion, "and on this basis start antireligious propaganda in the Tolstoy museums."

The schools were drawn more and more into the struggle

against the kulaks and the organization of collectives. The teachers had to explain the difference between kulaks and bedniaks in theory and illustrate it by comparisons between the children of poor peasants and those of priests in the class. Our committee on admissions, which consisted not only of the administration of the school but also of members of the party, the Komsomol cell, and the local Soviet, made it difficult for us to admit the children of kulaks or of the "servers of cult." One of the duties of the teacher of agriculture was to help the party and the Komsomol cell to forward the propaganda and the organizing of collective farms.

Some of the museum workers, without perceiving it, were drifting away from Tolstoy's ideas, or giving a one-sided picture of them. They described him as a revolutionary who opposed tsarism and the Orthodox church; but they said nothing about his nonresistance, his pacifism, his Christianity, his abhorrence of capital punishment and terrorism.

A circular from the Commissariat of Education suggested that the schools stay open Easter Sunday. I wanted to observe the day as usual, and I called a meeting of the teachers to make sure of their support.

To my surprise all but two voted against me, including my closest friends. In vain I spoke against separating the children from their families on that day, opposing the wishes of the parents and so creating antagonism between the school and the parents. The teachers were terrorized. Yet I knew that many of them, closing their doors and windows, would paint eggs and bake *kulichs* and *paskhas* for their children on that day!

I felt bitter at heart.

"Comrades," I said, "until now you have had faith in me, and believed that I could lead the school in a spirit of independence and freedom. You followed me and helped me. Now I feel that you no longer trust me, and I cannot work with you any more."

I could not speak, and left the room. This seemed the last straw. I felt that I was alone, that I was losing the support of my most devoted helpers.

The spring was late in 1929. The ice melted slowly on the rivers, and meadows and fields were full of water. I got up early in the morning and walked through the forest to my father's grave. It was still dark; the sun was just beginning to touch the tree tops. A thin crust of ice cracked, and water gurgled under my feet. I sat on a bench near the grave. There was no sound. Then, as the gold in the trees spread and brightened, a bird twittered and suddenly the woods were vibrant with singing. Here there was peace. All the rest was falsehood, and I had created it in my father's name.

The sun was high when I started home. I did not think, did not decide, but I *knew* that I could not go on living a lie.

LIX

THE BREAK

I HANDED in my resignation as director of the Yasnaia Poliana schools to the Department of Socialist Education. It was not accepted. I went to Moscow, saw the Acting Commissar of Education, Epstein, and told him that I could not go on.

"Why not?"

"I do not agree with the government's policy."

"For example?"

"I am against the forced collectivization of the peasants."

"We are not forcing them."

"You are creating such conditions that those who do not want to join the collectives are obliged to. Ignorant members of the party are not only 'curving the line' but ruining people. Not long ago in a village near us, a peasant left a collective, and the Communist cell refused to give him back his property. He had lost everything and was so desperate that he hanged himself!"

"I have just come from the country," Comrade Epstein said. "I visited several collectives. The peasants are all satisfied. They are using tractors, they have bought purebred cattle . . ."

"Where were you? Who told you this?"

"Oh, I went to various places. The peasants told me how happy they were, and, of course, no one knew who I was."

It was another case of not wishing to see the truth—eating caviar and believing that everyone ate it.

I was silent. It was useless to tell Comrade Epstein that a peasant could recognize him a mile away, and that every time he came to Yasnaia Poliana the whole population knew it.

"Please let me resign. I cannot continue working at the Educational Experiment Station of Yasnaia Poliana."

Epstein smiled.

"No, we can't dismiss you—we need you."

In March I petitioned the government to let me go abroad.

"Let me go to Japan for three months to study the schools, and perhaps to America. Then I can come back and work with new energy. I am very tired," I said to Mousey Solomonovich.

"Why do you want to go to Japan?"

"Because you won't let me go to Europe. There are too many *émigrés* there. It would be difficult for me not to see friends and relatives. And even if you let me go to Europe, and I saw no one, the G.P.U. would accuse me of being in touch with White Russians. There are scarcely any *émigrés* in Japan."

Everyone at Yasnaia Poliana asked me, "Will you come back, Alexandra Lvovna?" I hinted to a few close friends that I might stay abroad until the end of Bolshevism. At once the rumor spread that I was not coming back. The President of the Tula Executive Committee said, searching me with his eyes:

"You will certainly not come back. If I were in the place of the central authorities, I should never let you go."

"Aren't the institutions to which I have given so much of my energy sufficient guarantee for you, Comrade Stepanov?" I asked.

I no longer cared about the work at Yasnaia Poliana. And the chief work of the Tolstoy Society was done. The manuscripts had been sorted and copied, and most of the editorial work was finished. The publishing of this small edition of one thousand copies in Russian only did not interest me; it was a drop in the bucket. At three hundred rubles a set, who but commissars or foreigners could buy it? Even during the old *régime,* millions of copies had been printed in penny editions, which could be bought by the poorest people in Russia!

The G.P.U. repeatedly refused to give me a foreign passport, but for eight months I kept on trying. At the same time I was corresponding with several people in Japan, and toward the end of the summer, I received a cablegram inviting me to deliver a series of lectures in Tokyo, Osaka, and other big cities. With this, I went to one of the Soviet officials:

"If you will not let me go," I said, "I shall have to reply that I cannot accept because the Soviet authorities are afraid to let me go abroad."

When at last I held in my hands the red passport book with a crooked photograph of myself on the first page, I still did not believe that I should be able to go. The Commissariat of Education insisted on seeing the outline of my lectures and, after going over them, forbade my speaking about the Soviet schools. Books, letters, an address book, and manuscripts had to be taken to the commissariat for inspection. Then they were sealed so that I could not put anything more in the package.

It was difficult to get a permit to take my guitar with me. It was an old instrument, made by a famous craftsman.

"We do not let works of art go out of Russia," they told me. But I knew that art treasures from the Tsar's palace were constantly being sent abroad. "Why do you want a guitar, if you are only going for three months?"

"I take it with me wherever I go."

"All right, you may take it, if you promise to bring it back when you return to Russia."

It was an easy promise to make.

I said goodbye as I would if I were going away for a short time.

"But you will come back?" old Ilya Vasilievich asked.

"Of course I will, Ilya Vasilievich. Take care of yourself while I am away. Don't think of dying!"

"Please come back as quickly as possible."

The old man was crying.

I left late at night. A few friends got up to see me off. As Russian custom required, we all sat down. There was silence in the room. Some one sobbed. . . . I could not speak.

My ancient shabby carriage was brought to the front door. One of the team was old Osman. From the Volkonsky house where I lived we drove through the orchard to the highway, avoiding the main house. That was best—not to see, not to think—to break away quickly . . .

INDEX